Praying *for the* Impossible

How to Pray and Get a Miracle at all Cost!

By Uebert Snr Angel PhD

SpiritLibrary PUBLICATIONS

Unless otherwise stated, all scripture quotations are taken from the King James Version of the Bible.

ISBN 978-0-955 8116-2-3

Copyright 2012 by Uebert Snr Angel

Published by *SpiritLibrary* **Publications**

Printed in the United Kingdom of Great Britain. All rights reserved under International Copyright law. Contents and or cover may not be reproduced in whole or in part in any form without the express written consent of the publisher

Contents

Chapter One:
When you must have a miracle at all cost 5

Chapter Two:
SUPPLICATION - Requests and Arguments 23

Chapter Three:
Supplication – Gaining access to supplicate
– Approach, Attitudes, Gestures and Words 57

Chapter Four:
Men of Prayer who used supplication
- deesis - and got Miracles at all cost 77

Chapter Five:
Write your own Petition - deesis 87

CHAPTER ONE

When you must have a miracle at all cost

John Fletcher, an English Clergyman and author stained the walls of his room by the breath of his prayers. Smith Wigglesworth prayed until the glory smoke became visible and people convicted to the extent of running outside of the church building until he was done. Victor Kusi Boateng under extreme burden to preach to the whole world, yet knowing not a word in English prayed and fasted for a whole year and God supernaturally touched his tongue and he just woke up one day speaking perfect English.

St. Patrick moved by the plight of a family and deeply desiring to prove the power of Christ to some souls prayed for a corpse, six months in the grave, and it came back to life.

What of John Edwards who prayed until his hearers received prevenient grace from God, apart from which they would not have listened to his stern sweep of power on their souls? As it was, before John Edwards' hurricane filled words, thousands would collapse and those who remained on their seats were seen clinging to the edge of their seats, afraid of falling into the innermost depths of hell itself, literally.

Praying for the Impossible

Harry Ironside was one simple but prayerful man who understood how to pray for the impossible. In its early days, Dallas Theological Seminary was in critical need of thousands of dollars to keep the work going. During a prayer meeting, renowned Bible teacher Harry Ironside, a lecturer at the school, impregnated by the revelation of praying for the impossible prayed,

"Lord, you own the cattle on a thousand hills. Please sell some of those cattle to help us meet this need."

Just hours after the prayer, a cheque for the exact thousands they needed arrived at the school, Harry Ironside asked the man what prompted him to give and the man said He had just sold cattle from his farm. Ironside called out to his prayer partner, "…hey God has sold the cattle…!"

Such was the prayer life of these men that they were determined to have a miracle at all cost. They knew the secrets and they knew the order, they knew how to get a miracle at all cost. You can be like them today!

It's a choice

You can choose to learn how to pray for the impossible until you are God plated and God enamored. It is possible. It is achievable to have 100% guaranteed answer to prayer. You can have a miracle at all cost but you need to know the correct way to pray for the impossible and have the deep anointing of Jacob who wrestled with God and cried out:

**...I won't let go until you bless me.
Genesis 32 vs.26**

As aforementioned, God is a God of order and does everything in order, so these times when we must have a miracle at all cost require and call for us to adhere to prayer guidelines and if we are ignorant of the guidelines we will not have a miracle. It is THAT simple!

The visitation from the Lord

This is exactly what the Lord taught me in a visitation on the 21st of December 2011 on the second day of our 12-day fast. That day I expected nothing to happen just like I did not expect to be the first man to land on the moon but from nowhere a deep sensation ran down my spine and the Lord entered the room and without introduction he spoke on *how Christians are ignorant of the order of prayer and how they are ignorant of the fact that there is such a thing as a prayer for the impossible.*

I was shocked at the revelation and the verse of scripture he revealed to me was very familiar to my spirit but I did not know the real meaning. I quickly ran to where my bible was and opened it and there it was:

**I exhort therefore, that, FIRST OF ALL, SUPPLICATIONS, prayers, intercessions and giving of thanks, be done for all man...
1 Timothy 2 vs. 1**

The Lord began to tell me that the scripture opens up the kind of prayer we must do first. He expounded that many believers just pray haphazardly with no clear order, yet God has already given the order and the right way of getting a miracle. He said, "Doesn't my word say…"

**…God looks over his word to perform it…
Ezekiel 12 vs.25**

He also said,

**…God who seeks counsel of his will (word)
Ephesians 1 vs.11.**

This was like a light bulb lighting up in my spirit and things became somewhat clearer, but only for a moment since I thought I knew what supplications was.

The Lord said,
"Do you see that all these words are plural and that they start with supplications?"

I had not checked this and it was a new thing to me. This meant that all these prayers can be done many times except the prayer of faith where repetition is the badge of doubt.

The Lord told me that many times in my life he had prompted me without my actually realizing it, to use the revelation on praying for the impossible which he was now imploring me to use. He told me these times it was his grace that led me to praying and getting a miracle at all cost without me even realizing which kind of prayer I was using.

My office was now condensed with Glory smoke and my body seemed to be jumping off my skin in awe of the Lord and the revelation of praying for the impossible. I could not contain the revelation and I wanted to get someone to tell this revelation to as soon as possible. It was like a man who finds treasure and secures it. I wanted to start praying this prayer and at the same time knew how difficult it was to explain this revelation. I also knew there were other types of prayer that people needed to be taught.

Now, the Lord told of a visit he had paid me before this instance but according to him, I was too engaged in a lot of things so was not ready to receive the revelation. In ministry it's easy to be busy doing God's work that you might not really give God himself time to speak about your personal life. Especially in the prophetic office where I am, you can be busy telling others what God said about their lives that you don't get time to hear what God is saying about yours. So I understood completely what God was saying. I was too busy telling people what God was saying about them that I was no longer listening to everything he was saying to me and this was a wake up call. However, God's mercy got me a miracle even before the full revelation came.

When all hope was lost and hope far away God, through the revelation in this book gave me a miracle when I needed it the most!

A Time I needed a Miracle

This revelation of praying for the impossible came at a time when I was in deep waters financially in my television ministry. Beverly and I had just launched Miracle TV and it needed thousands upon thousands of dollars to keep it afloat. In fact at the time, we were in the red since this channel is funded solely by my wife and I.

When this revelation came, Miracle TV was literally on its knees yet there was no one to turn to or may I say I did not want to ask for money from those who could have helped. You see for faith to grow, many times you don't need to accept a lot of handouts and with five days left for the channel to be closed for non payment, I became very desperate in my spirit to get a supernatural answer. My spirit began to get information from on high on a better way of getting a miracle at all cost but I was not getting the whole revelation. My spirit knew there was a way but with five days left it was now despairing.

You see, there are many prayers one can pray as stated in 1 Timothy 2 vs.1;

I exhort therefore, that, first of all, supplications, PRAYERS, intercessions and giving of thanks, be done for all man...

Did you see that? Timothy says there are PRAYERS meaning to say these are many. Now, I don't mean to be dogmatic but I had used all the prayers I knew how to pray and had fasted all I knew how to fast but it seemed there was just no answer. The miracle was nowhere to be found and soon the five days left became two days. I was still trusting God but this was a problem. He was the one who had said we should start Miracle TV and now it seemed as if there was no answer coming.

AND that's when it happened. PRAYING FOR THE IMPOSSIBLE…How to pray and get a Miracle at all cost!

God invaded earth for my sake and spoke clearly and I followed the guidelines he gave me as outlined in this book and days later, on the actual day the TV Station was supposed to be shut down money came. I was just called to the office and a couple had brought two separate seeds that amounted to the EXACT amount I needed!

No one knew how much we needed, let alone the fact that we needed money at all. We just did not tell anyone. No one knew but God!

Notice that this book is not trying to cancel other types of prayer or undermine them for that would be diabolic. All I am highlighting is a kind of prayer stated in the Bible that you pray when the situation is desperate and when you must get a miracle at all cost. I have done it and it works every time and yet I still use other kinds of prayer also as the word commands me to do.

I will just highlight some of the types of prayers for you to have knowledge of when they are necessary then I will get back to the subject of praying for the the impossible. Stay with me here!

The Order and Types of Prayer

Before we go to where the rubber meets the steel, it is good that we see in a nutshell the other types of prayers that are in the word.

1 **Timothy 2 vs. 1** is very instructive in the choice of sentence structure and semantics used by Apostle Paul.

The words **'first of all'** denote a prescribed order to prayer for we are dealing with four types of prayer here, among many others but they are in a certain order. First **supplications**, second **prayers**, third **intercessions** and fourth the **giving of thanks**. Our God is a God of order and he has a certain way which he operates in. The onus is on us to understand that order and use it to achieve the impossible. Also notice the prayers are in plural form which means they can be prayed collectively or individually and they could be prayed multiple times. In other words you can pray them over and over again. Some prayers like the prayer of faith or the prayer of agreement you pray one time and that is enough. Multiple prayers over a prayer of faith will imply an inborn element of doubt or little or weak faith.

Not appreciating the different types of prayer will hinder your prayer life. If you recognize the prayer of faith only, you may fail to intercede for a child or friend who has gone astray or needs God to intervene.

Types of prayer

Prayer of Faith

Essentially all prayer relies on our faith in God but the prayer of faith is rooted in our confidence in God's word. Such prayers are done once and that settles it, hence any doubts will short circuit the power of your prayer. After such prayers you must immediately act upon what you believe. Unlike intercession where the prayer point may be out of your focus of control you may have to keep praying until you receive a note of victory in your spirit. With prayers of faith, repeated prayers over the same thing are a sure sign of doubt. You ask only once, believe it has been established and thereafter when you pray about the same thing it is just thanksgiving.

I remember a gentleman I ministered to a few years ago who had a very serious case of sugar diabetes. He told of how he had spent so many years praying almost every day for the disease to go to no avail. He had come to a point of giving up on prayer. I then briefly went over what a prayer of faith meant and how it was going to bring about his healing based on what the word of God says. The man immediately went on his knees and prayed a simple prayer of faith. He stood up immediately and by faith began to declare that he was healed. A month later the man came to church wielding results from the hospital that cleared him of any trace of diabetes in his system, what a God we serve! He happily testified that after the day he prayed a prayer of faith, he kept thanking God for healing every day until the day he went back to the hospital for further tests. That is what the prayer of faith can do. The word of God says in the book of Mark 11 vs. 24;

You shall have what you say...

The prayer of faith simply calls for action on what you prayed for and on what you believe. Like the woman with the issue of blood, her faith defied cultural norms and she forced her way through the crowd and forcefully grabbed the hem of Jesus' garment. In response Jesus said;

...your faith has made you well...
Mark 5 vs. 26-34.

Such a prayer is made primarily to a person's own life – to his situations, circumstances and desires. It is not talking about someone else praying with you. You see, God has given us all free will. So your prayer of faith will not always work for others because the other persons will and faith enters into the picture as well.

Prayer of Agreement

This type of prayer is very straightforward. When two or more people with a common matter or issue come together and agree with one another and with the word of God that something specific will be done. It's a call for unity with one purpose, sharing a joint vision and God's power will be released. The agreement brings more faith into action.

A woman once came to my wife and I and asked us to pray a prayer of agreement with her so that her lover who was a married man would divorce his wife! No, no, it does not work that way. Before you pray this prayer with your prayer partner or your spouse, always make sure what you want to agree on is in line with God's word.

The word of God says in the book of Matthew;

If two people bind anything on earth…it is bound in heaven
Matthew 18 vs.18-19

Prayer of Dedication or Consecration
This is a humble submission to the will of God; it means placing your desires and wants below the will of God. It is about asking for strength to accomplish his will by his power.

Luke 22 vs. 39-42 gives us an account of such a prayer made by The Lord Jesus Christ in the garden of Gethsemane. It was very short,

Father, if it is your will, take this cup away from Me; nevertheless not My will, but Yours, be done.

This prayer was earnest and done in agony to the extent that His sweat became like great drops of blood. He knew God's will but he prayed a prayer of consecration, for he was not praying to change the situation but to submit to God's will. There are some instances in your life as a believer where you need to establish first the will of God concerning your life and how do you do that? Get acquainted to his word! Once you have done that, humbly submit to that perfect purpose he has for you – that is a prayer of dedication or consecration.

However when it comes to changing a situation you might be in and receiving blessings from God according to his word, we do not pray, 'if it be thy will'. We already know God's will because we have it in the word, it is God's will that our needs be met and we receive our needs by using the prayer of faith.

Prayer of Penitence or Repentance – this essentially is asking God for forgiveness of sin. By confessing our sins we are acknowledging that we missed the mark and are repentant. An unconfessed sin is a major obstacle to an authentic and intimate relationship with God. As a believer always have a repentant spirit that is quick to recognize your mistakes.

…contrite spirit…

The book of **Psalm 51 says;**

Have mercy upon me oh God according to thy loving kindness
According unto the multitude of thy tender mercies blot out my transgressions

Wash me thoroughly from mine iniquity and cleanse me from my sin…for thou desirest not sacrifice else would I give it thou delightest not in burnt offering. The sacrifices of God are a *broken (contrite)* spirit.
Psalm 51 vs. 1-2, 16-17

Prayer of Praise and Worship

This prayer is centered upon God and His eternal characteristics – His majesty, glory, beauty, love, mercy, grace and power. Ever had a time when you just broke into a song or psalm of praise and/or worship? When you just found yourself just adoring God in prayer? That is what is called a prayer of praise and worship. My wife and I often spend time just speaking to him about how truly good he is, how amazing it is to sit at his feet and experience his glory and his tangible anointing just flowing through. It is important for all who call themselves children of the Most High God to pray this prayer and experience him through it. This may even form the beginning or part of another type of prayer. Such a prayer can be found in the book of **1 Chronicles 29 vs. 10-13.** David says;

...blessed be thou, Lord God of Israel our father, forever and ever. Thine, O Lord, is the greatness, and the power, and the glory, and the victory and the majesty: for all that is in the heaven and in the earth is thine; thine is the kingdom, O Lord, and thou art exalted as head above all...

Now therefore, our God, we thank thee, and praise thy glorious name.

Prayer of meditation

The prayer of meditation is a prayer that involves deep pondering or murmuring on God's word, it's about filling your spirit with God's word, personalizing His word and downloading it into your spirit. It's about renewing your mind, matching it with God's will and purpose for you. It could be soul searching about a particular question you have and waiting upon a response in your spirit. Meditation also involves erasing beliefs, cultures, traditions and subconscious patterns that cause disease, failure and stress which rob you of your joy and blessings in Christ. Many a time believers all over the world find themselves in difficult situations that do not line up with the word of God because of culture or tradition.

The prayer of meditation allows you to venture deeper into a walk with God that far surpasses the confines of bad tradition or culture, changing your perception, views and ultimately changing you as you line up with the mindset of Christ. The word of God says you should meditate on his word day and night as seen in the book of **Joshua 1 vs. 8**

This book of law shall not depart out of thy mouth, but thou shalt meditate therein day and night, that thou mayest observe to do according to all that is written therein, for then thou shalt make thy way prosperous, and then thou shall have good success.

Notice, the prayer of meditation also makes way for prosperity and not just prosperity but *good* success.

There are also other types of prayers like **Prayer of Authority** - over the devil by binding or loosing, casting out and **praying in tongues** and **Fasting and Praying** which will need another complete book to explore. Others include prayer of forgiveness, and prayer of fellowship among others.

Prayer of Intercessions

To intercede means to plead or mediate on behalf of another person, it is essentially standing in the gap in prayer on behalf of another. It is also in plural form which means it is not a one off prayer, one can pray relentlessly over the issue. When we take it upon ourselves to pray earnestly for other people we enter into the realm of intercession. To enter into that realm we must have a heart that really loves the Lord and cares about the things God cares about. It's no longer about yourself or your needs but you are now standing in the gap for someone, a church or even a country so you are being sincere and sensitive about issues that affect others.

As a Prophet there are so many instances where God will show me things about different countries (from weather warnings to economics), dignitaries, celebrities, ordinary people and various corporations. As he permits, I often share these things with my congregation and as a church we intercede for those that God tells us to. There is power to cause change when believers come together to intercede for others. In the book of Genesis chapter 18 vs. 22-33; Abraham stood before God and interceded for the people of Sodom as God was going to annihilate them.

...and Abraham drew near and he said, wilt thou destroy the righteous with the wicked?...

This is a good example of a prayer of intercession.

Praying for the Impossible

Giving of thanks

The last type of prayer I would like to highlight before going back into supplication is the prayer of giving thanks. The core of thanksgiving is acknowledging God for who he is. Thanking God for whatever He has done keeps us focused on him as our only source of strength. Giving thanks to God always shows your humility. You will be acknowledging that it's not by your own power or might but by the spirit of the Lord that you are progressing in life. This prayer is giving God glory for whatever he has, is and will continue to do in your life and should be punctuated with praise and worship.

1 Thessalonians 5 vs. 16-18 puts it this way;
Rejoice evermore. Pray without ceasing. In everything give thanks for this is the will of God in Christ Jesus concerning you.

In the book of Acts 16, Paul and Silas sang praises unto the Lord even though they were bound in prison. They did not look at their present circumstances in order for them to praise and give God thanks and it resulted in them being freed from prison.

I read one time about a woman who lay motionless on her death bed and the saints from her church including family and friends all took turns to pray over her every hour for what seemed to be months on end. After praying for her for so long with no change, the people started growing wearier and wearier as the woman slipped further and further into unconsciousness.

While everyone sat and prayed seemingly tired one night, the pastor suddenly jumped up from his chair and told everyone to sing praises to the Lord. He had gotten the revelation. So they all stood up and started singing praises to the Lord as if something great had just happened. It was not long before the woman opened her eyes, sat up in bed and asked for something to eat as if nothing had happened to her. She was completely healed that night through the prayer of giving thanks.

There are some situations where instead of crying out to God for a solution to your problem, give Him thanks, rejoicing always and not being phased by what the devil throws at you. This kind of prayer can be used as part of another kind of prayer and it gets you results!

A few scriptures to note that pertain to thanksgiving are as follows;

Psalm 95:2 - Let us come into his presence with thanksgiving; let us make a joyful noise to him with praise.

Ephesians 5:20 - Giving thanks always, for all things, to God the Father in the name of our Lord Jesus Christ

1 Thessalonians 5:18 - In everything give thanks; for this is the will of God in Christ Jesus

Hebrews 13:15 - Therefore, let us continually offer to God the sacrifice of praise, that is, the fruit of our lips, giving thanks to His name."

Psalm 97:12 - Rejoice in the Lord, and give thanks.

Back to Supplication

Now, let's look on the prayer for the impossible because this is the main focus of this book. I want miracles to come to you at all cost.

See, I have heard a lot of people saying; "your miracle is around the corner" yet they never show us the corner. To such I have always had a problem. If my miracle is around the corner show me the corner and I will go to the corner myself and collect my own miracle! I tell you this revelation will show you the corner. In fact THE PRAYER OF SUPPLICATION is the corner.

However you need to understand all that is involved in this SUPPLICATION. Never reason that you already know what it is because that was my problem too until the Lord taught me.

Supplication

You should keep in mind before we go any further and before you try to understand how to pray and get a miracle at all cost, the word 'supplication' is in a legal format. I want you to really get this as I explain.

Now, the word of God is a legal document hence the use of the words **'testament'** and **'will'** this is why many words are put in legal format. In order to then understand how to pray for the impossible one should understand the legal guidelines involved because SUPPLICATION itself is a very legal word (In fact more legal than most of the words in scripture). That makes the prayer of SUPPLICATION, a legal thing that relies on a lot of elements that when grasped they usher the one praying into a wave of miracles.

When you must have a miracle at all cost

So defining supplication in a nutshell - Supplication in the broad and loose sense means 'petition', In legal terms supplication is defined as 'A formal request addressed to an official person, or to an organized body, having power to grant it.

In the ancient Greek and Roman societies the relation between supplication and the Legal systems is crucial to the developmental aspect of praying for the impossible. Supplication as a legal process consists of three steps;

1. An approach made by the suppliant, (the person pleading their case, i.e. you)
2. His use of a gesture or word in his presentation of request, and
3. A response by the party entertaining the request, known as the supplicantus or in the prayer of supplications case, GOD.

The Romans also used supplication as a form of appeal against mistaken verdicts and as a means of rectifying inadequate legislation.

I will draw your attention to the use of the word supplication in the Bible.

The word supplication or supplications is used 60 times in the Bible in 58 verses. The words pray or prayers are used together with it in 31 of those verses. Seven times supplication is used with the words crying out to the Lord and three times it used together with weeping.

One person can make supplication to another person. A man kneeling before a woman to propose marriage is supplicating.

Three times in the Bible it is used of someone petitioning the king, another time a delegation brings supplication to Jeremiah, and there is a prophecy of the heathen nations making supplication to Israel. One can beseech another man of good standing before God to supplicate on their behalf as seen in Jeremiah 42; 1-9. Let me further expand on the word supplication for further understanding.

Supplication as a WORD

Supplication is related to the word *supple*. It also refers to bending of the knees, which denotes humility and honour. The word means that literally or figuratively a person falls down on their knees in prayer before God. We have an example of this in a prayer in which Solomon uses the word supplication ten times:

And so it was, when Solomon had finished praying all this prayer and supplication to the LORD, that he arose from before the altar of the LORD, from kneeling on his knees with his hands spread up to heaven.
1 Kings 8 vs. 54 NKJV

This book will give you a revelation on how to pray for the impossible and achieve a miracle at all cost. The key is this very same supplication and we are going to look at what it means further in order to get a better understanding. We will look at how we supplicate in humility, the gestures and attitudes involved, how to gain access and then finally look at examples from the bible of how men of God applied supplication and achieved the impossible

CHAPTER TWO

SUPPLICATION - Requests and Arguments

1 Timothy 2 vs.1
I exhort therefore, that, FIRST OF ALL, SUPPLICATIONS, prayers, intercessions and giving of thanks, be made for all men,

For us to really understand fully what supplication is, we have to understand that Apostle Paul uses two legal words in the scripture above which shows us the intensity and severity of the matter at hand. We are not being asked or encouraged here but we are being ordered, implored, beseeched, exhorted not only to follow the order but to start with supplications In our requests to God, do you see that?

The first legal word mentioned by Apostle Paul in this passage of scripture to Timothy is **exhort.** It comes from the Greek root word **parakaleo**, which means to summon or to order an individual to appear before a court. Therefore we are being summoned to stand before the court of heaven in order to supplicate as if in a court system. Right here I just pray for you to see where this is taking you! This is the meat of the gospel and the very same reason why some of you have done marathons in prayer yet have nothing to show for it.

Apostle Paul in a way says this is not an option that is why he is using the word parakaleo or summon because there is just no option here. Its either you follow or you receive the consequences.

He says:

"I exhort…"

He is standing here like a sheriff giving summons that need to be responded to. He has a legal document binding and strong, commanding us to **deesis** or SUPPLICATE if we want a miracle at all cost. This is a must and not an option! Boy I love Jesus!

The second legal word in the first book of Timothy 2 vs.1 is supplication which is from the Greek root word ***deesis***, which means a petition, entreaty or request.

Supplication is a word used in the legal system to represent a formal written application carrying evidence requesting a court for a specific legal action. It is a well-written document requesting a right or benefit from a person in authority to change the course of things.

You see how lost many Christians are with regards to supplication? Some don't even know that the word supplication exists. Some know there is supplication but they really don't know how to supplicate. Some think they know what it is and still some confuse supplication for general prayer or intercession.

Even some Christian and non Christian dictionaries and commentaries get it all wrong and as a result many believers are financially broke, spiritually bankrupt, physically busted, emotionally downtrodden and walk defeated because they have not found the way to pray a prayer that can make them get 100% answer to prayer. God has the answer and it's called supplication. It is *deesis*.

Now listen, I want to show you how to pray a prayer of supplication which the Lord showed me will get you a miracle at all cost. I have tested it many times and have taught many to follow it and they are enjoying the results.

How Supplication (deesis) is Done

Now since praying for the impossible includes words that are in the legal system we have to understand how it all works in the legal system.

Those who have worked or been to court will understand that in a court system your plea stands and falls based upon its merit or evidence. This applies as well to praying for the impossible using the prayer of supplication; your request has to carry great merits for it to be heard. The merits should be founded on the word and presented as arguments as done in the practice of courts where a case is on trial.

For a supplication to carry merit it should have a strong case or argument otherwise you run the risk that not only will the supplication not be heard but also your prayers may not even be considered under supplication criteria.

Praying for the Impossible

Just take a look at this…

Psalm 6 vs. 9
The Lord has heard my supplications; The Lord will receive my prayer.

Now, this emphasizes not only the order but importance of merits. For David to say,

"The Lord has heard my supplications"

It means it is possible that supplications may not be entertained due to poor merits or evidence which therefore will result in the supplications being thrown out the same way a case is thrown out of court before a judge. Also notice, the Lord received his prayer only after the supplications had been heard which makes the order a priority. Did you see that he says; "the Lord has heard my supplications so he will receive my prayer". David says since God heard my supplication then my prayer will be accepted by God. See there is order here, deesis or supplication first and then prayer gets answered.

Stay with the word here and you will see how you will pray for the impossible.

The Word of God is your evidence and your merit

For a supplication to carry strong merits, the argument should be based on God's written word (logos) or promise. This is done by bringing him into remembrance of his own written word *(logos)* or promise which may have come as a *rhema (spoken)* word either by prophecy or a spoken word. This is all consistent with the court system where a petition or appeal is based on a written law or constitutional right.

However the argument in supplication must be presented in humility, honour and with a submissive heart and in order.

The order is equally important, as emphasized by the words;

"...*first of all...*"

Unfortunately many people's prayer lives are out of order and lack the requirements of a supplication, which is why they simply do not work. We serve a God of order who has placed his word in a legal format since he is the Great judge, the devil; a great accuser and Jesus A GREAT mediator or lawyer and you are the accused. If you are not aware of this legal system in the spiritual realm you will not get a miracle no matter how you try unless it is by God's act of charity or benevolence.

Watch this about the Judge and Advocate;

To the general assembly and church of the firstborn, which are written in heaven, and to God the JUDGE OF ALL, and to the spirits of just men made perfect, And to Jesus the MEDIATOR of the new covenant, and to the blood of sprinkling, that speaketh better things than that of Abel.
Hebrews 12 vs. 23-24.

And of the accuser;
And the Great dragon was cast out, that old serpent, called the Devil, and Satan, which deceiveth the whole world, he was cast out into the earth, and his angels were cast out with him. And I heard a loud voice saying in heaven, Now is come salvation, and strength, and the kingdom of our God, and the power of his Christ; for the ACCUSER of our brethren (YOU) is cast down, which accused them before our God day and night. Revelation 12 vs. 9-10.

Legal Arguments

Now here is where we start!

The legal process of the court hearings here on earth where the Lord has placed us bears striking resemblance to how we are able to present our arguments in supplications to the Lord. Keep in mind God is the GREAT JUDGE, the devil; a great accuser and Jesus A GREAT mediator or lawyer and you are the accused.

A legal argument like in supplicating before the Lord should carry five core points. This is what these five points look like in a legal system on earth today, (note that I have written a much simpler version of these core points soon after this)

1 **Statement of conclusion by applicant** – specify your appeal or opposing prior judgment;

2. **A statement of the rule that supports the conclusion** – citation of the cornerstone argument against prior judgment or cornerstone of appeal;
3. **Proof of the rule through citation to authority, through explanations of how the authority stands for the rule, through analyses of policy, and through counter-analyses** – detailed citation of the relevant legal instruments, which support your appeal or opposition to prior judgment.
4. **Application of the rule's elements to the facts with the aid of supporting authority, policy considerations, and counter-analyses, thus completing proof of the conclusion** – application of the detailed proof or evidence cited and more importantly connecting it with precedent cases relevant to the matter on hand. Showing how judgment passed in those precedent cases is inconsistent with the case being appealed.
5. **Cross examination of witnesses** – the opportunity to ask questions in court of a witness who has testified in a trial

Don't get bogged down by the terms here. It will make sense in a while and as you read this you will understand these points and how to apply them to your situation in a way that is very simple. You will get a miracle at all cost!

Here are the five points laid down to you in a very simple way and in connection to how you use them in the prayer of supplication:

In the context of supplication – deesis;

1. **Statement of conclusion by applicant** - This is your prayer request, that which you have prayed day and night and because of no solution now deem impossible, that which you desire a miracle at all cost.
2. **A statement of the rule that supports the conclusion** - This is when you support your prayer request with Gods promise or word about you or how God sees you.
3. **Proof of the rule through citation to authority** - This is when you cite or mention the relevant scriptures, which give you the right or grace to appeal, contend, reason or argue your case with God.
4. **Application of the rule's elements to the facts** - This is when you show cause the basis of your request of a miracle at all cost, linking it to the relevant scriptures which concern your issue and showing how your situation is inconsistent with Gods promise concerning you.
5. **Cross examination** - This is your opportunity to call upon examples of people you know or in the bible who have experienced breakthrough in the same case as yours.

This you will only find by reading, searching and meditating upon the word of God. Then you write them down as part of your supplication. If the word in you is weak, your capacity to supplicate will be compromised.

However the supplication even though based on the word should be presented in humility. This is not an exercise of pride. It is a humble exercise. It is no excuse that God is the one who called us to reason with him. God says we can reason with him or give our supplication or present merits from his words to him out of his love for us. So when we reason with him we are supposed to really know that God's grace allowed us the ability to reason with him.

The bible puts it this way,

Come now, and let us reason together, saith the lord. Isaiah 1 vs. 18

This is the Almighty himself inviting you to come and reason with Him, to bring forth your petitions, your supplications. This is the same invite granted in the book of **Hebrews 4 vs. 16**;

Come boldly unto the throne of grace that we may obtain mercy, and find grace to help in time of need.

Therefore come boldly with your reasons in supplication. Tell God what you have found in his word and prove how it's contrary to what the devil is throwing at you. Show God you have a strong case based upon the promises in his word. You do this by sitting down with yourself and searching the scriptures and writing the ones that cover your situation. In God's case you win when you bring to him what he has said.

God wants us to bring our cases to him based on the word he has spoken. He is willing to answer a prayer based on evidence.

See **Isaiah 41 vs. 21**

Produce your case, saith the lord, bring forth your strong reasons saith the king of Jacob.

Your case should carry evidence and strong reasons for it to be heard. Failure of which, it will be thrown out, remember;

James 4 vs. 3
Ye ask, and receive not, because ye ask amiss, that ye may consume it upon your lusts

In supplications, coming forth with weak reasons is equal to asking amiss which is why people do not receive. It's as good as singing twinkle twinkle little star and hoping to get a miracle afterwards. The Lord said people are not praying through because of this ignorance. They are not willing to follow what I said through **Isaiah 43 vs. 26;**
Put me in remembrance, let us plead (contend, argue, reason) together; declare then that might be justified (acquitted/released) AMP

Notice the legal language used in the three scriptures – case, plea, strong reasons, acquitted.

The invite to pray a prayer of supplication calls for you to be able to bring Him into remembrance of his word as one before a court system may give citation to a constitution or Act as a way of appealing a case. Your strong reasons or arguments will determine if you will be acquitted, justified or in our context if our supplication will be heard.

This is the way believers are expected to give supplications if we are to pray for the impossible and get results.

So you need your supplications (deesis) to be;

Written, as prayer points as if you are preparing for a legal case.

The written supplication should carry strong reasons or arguments based on God's word, promises or deeds done as per God's word.

The strong arguments should be presented as a way of bringing God into remembrance, as in bringing his word back to him. Find scriptures that cover your case. This is done so as to give merits and strengthen your supplication. The arguments are always addressed to God as He is the Supreme Authority.

Your supplication should always be done in humility, respect and with honour the same way one that is before a court shows humility and respect to the Judge and court he is before. You might have heard people who have lost cases for being held in contempt. It simply means they were disrespectful of the courts authority. Same is true with supplication, respect God and be humble or else risk the possibility of being held in contempt.

Find examples of people you know who have experienced what you are going through and got their miracle, include them as part of your case building.

Men who have done these things became very close or were very close to God that they acted like they were part of the board members of heaven. They said things that would sound like heresy in today's world. They asked and questioned God in a way difficult for many to understand especially those that do not know supplication.

Think of men like Moses telling the Lord to repent. What about Abraham who negotiated with God. These men had the secret on how to get God to answer their prayers. They had the secret of supplication exercised on a daily basis.

Moses' supplication

...Repent from your anger...
Exodus 32 vs. 12

How is it possible for a man to say to God;

...repent from your anger...

What gave Moses such boldness and audacity to tell the creator to repent from his anger? The answer is simple when one becomes a person of **supplication (deesis)**, they are elevated to the 'boardroom' of heaven since they are a stickler to God's words. No one gets to pray for the impossible unless they are word people and take God's word as final authority, inerrant and sufficient in its nature. You must take God at his WORD!

This level or dimension requires one to be one with God's word and only then can you be quick to gather facts on what the word says and thereby getting the merits for whatever case you want to bring before the LORD.

If you look in the book of Exodus, the Prophet Moses, who was given the five books of the bible to pen, gives us a typical case of supplication to God where God is brought into remembrance of the prophets merits (his strong case, arguments) to God based on the covenant God entered with Abraham which Moses knew quite well since he read it and even wrote it.

Exodus 32 vs. 8;15

They have turned aside quickly out of the way which I commanded them: they have made them a molten calf, and have worshipped it, and have sacrificed thereunto, and said, These be thy gods, O Israel, which have brought thee up out of the land of Egypt. And the LORD said unto Moses, I have seen this people, and, behold, it is a stiff-necked people: Now therefore let me alone, that my wrath may wax hot against them, and that I may consume them: and I will make of thee a great nation.

And Moses besought † the LORD his God, and said, LORD, why doth thy wrath wax hot against thy people, which thou hast brought forth out of the land of Egypt with great power, and with a mighty hand? Wherefore should the Egyptians speak, and say, For mischief did he bring them out, to slay them in the mountains, and to consume them from the face of the earth? Turn from thy fierce wrath, and repent of this evil against thy people.

Praying for the Impossible

Remember Abraham, Isaac, and Israel, thy servants, to whom thou swarest by thine own self, and saidst unto them, I will multiply your seed as the stars of heaven, and all this land that I have spoken of will I give unto your seed, and they shall inherit it for ever. And the LORD repented of the evil which he thought to do unto his people. And Moses turned, and went down from the mount, and the two tables of the testimony were in his hand: the tables were written on both their sides; on the one side and on the other were they written.

Going back to our five legal principles that show you how to outline your prayer for the impossible, see how Moses did it in his day.

1 Statement of conclusion;
In our case the statement of conclusion (prayer request) is the first part and here Moses says;

"...turn from thy fierce wrath, and repent of this evil against thy people..."

This conclusion is the supplication of Moses to God. This was his request in a bid to save the children of Israel from God's wrath because of idol worshipping they had committed. This did not require the prayer of faith. It did not require intercession or the prayer of agreement. It required supplication for this was the best way to get a miracle at all cost. See all you do is read the word, outline your case and present it to a good judge who is God and the miracle is yours as long as the merits are from his word. Moses knew it and chose the thing and the way that could have given him a quick miracle and that was supplication, deesis.

However when you look at Moses' approach It appears bold and aggressive to ask God to repent if one does not understand their legal rights with God, one has to develop an intimate relationship with God founded on the word for one to have such boldness and legal standing to make such a deesis (supplication).

2 A statement of the rule that supports the conclusion
In humility Moses besought the Lord his God, and said Lord,

"why doth thy wrath wax hot against thy people which thou hast brought forth out of the land of Egypt with great power and with a mighty hand."

Also In a bid to support his conclusion or supplication Prophet Moses supports the conclusion by combining it with what the Lord had done for the children of Israel and what the Egyptians would say about the Lords wrath against the children of Israel.

"Wherefore should the Egyptians speak, and say, For mischief did he bring them out, to slay them in the mountains, and to consume them from the face of the earth?"

3. Proof of the rule through citation to authority and through explanation of how authority stands for the rule.

We notice Moses puts the Lord into remembrance, reasons together with the Lord by producing his case by referring to the covenant and promise God entered with Abraham and his descendants Isaac and Israel (Jacob).

The covenant is in the book of genesis…

Genesis 22 vs.16-18

'By Myself I have sworn, says the Lord, because you have done this thing, and have not withheld your only son – blessing I will bless you, and multiply I will multiply your descendants as the stars of the heaven and as the sand which is on the seashore, and your descendants shall possess the gate of their enemies. In your seed all the nations of the earth shall be blessed, because you have obeyed my voice'.

So one may ask, why is it important to give citation of God's word back to God…

Psalms 138 vs.2

I will worship toward thy holy temple, and praise thy name for thy loving-kindness and for thy truth: for thou hast magnified thy word above all thy name.
If God's word has been magnified above all it then means, his word has become a law unto him – this is the revelation Moses caught onto and which all believers have to get hold of. God cannot go against his word. It is that simple and its high time Christians used that 'loophole'.

Supplication - Requests and Arguments

Moses was aware of God's word on the promise and covenant he made with Abraham; in his supplication he made reference by way of bringing the Lord into remembrance of his very word.

As Psalms 138 vs.2 puts it, God himself has put his very word above himself yet in John 1 vs.1 God is revealed as the word, which means he cannot go against his own word for to do that is to go against himself.

The amplified version puts the very same scripture differently but in a way that highlights why supplication is the fastest way to get a miracle and the most guaranteed way of getting a miracle at all cost;

Put Me in remembrance [*remind Me of your merits*]; let us *plead and argue* together. Set forth your case, that you may be *justified (proved right, acquitted)* Isaiah 43 vs.26 AMP

The amplified version is right on point here. The key words highlighted are:
i. Remind me of your merits
ii. Plead and argue your case
iii. Justified, proved right or acquitted

4 Application of the rules elements to the facts with the aid of supporting authority.

Moses applied the covenant between God and Abraham to the facts on hand concerning the children of Israel, the authority being God's word or part of the covenant.

Praying for the Impossible

Essentially Moses' cornerstone authority was that the Lord God has placed His word above himself and he knew he was dealing with a covenant keeping God.

After Moses had presented his strong case this is how the covenant keeping God responded.

'And the Lord repented from the evil which he had thought to do to his people.'

Is this not amazing how God can respond to a prayer of supplication with just merits from a man who confessed he was inadequate and stammered for that matter. It was not Moses' good looks that got the prayer to be answered nor was it his voice projection or eloquence. Moses stammered. It was only his merits based on the word. Based on what God had already said. He used the 'loophole'…God respects his word for he is his word. You bring it back to him in supplication and he has no way out, per se.

5 Cross examination

Remember Abraham, Isaac, and Israel, thy servants, to whom thou swarest by thine own self, and saidst unto them, I will multiply your seed as the stars of heaven, and all this land that I have spoken of will I give unto your seed, and they shall inherit it forever.

In a similar fashion to fact four which deals with supporting authority, cross examination of people who have gone before is key with a prayer of supplication. It gives examples of actual people as Apostle Paul says in the book of **1 Corinthians 10 vs.11**

Now all these things happened unto them for ensamples; and they are written for our admonition...

There are things in the word of God that are simply there to show us by example actions we ought to take or not take in life. The word of God is one place to find actual events that match what you are going through today. This is what you use as part of your cross examination of evidence in a prayer of supplication.

Paul goes on to say;

Remember them which have the rule over you, who have spoken unto you the word of God: whose faith follow...
Hebrews 13 vs.7

So Apostle Paul is encouraging us to take examples from men of faith and follow them. Find a man or woman of God who can lead you by their example. In your prayer of supplication as part of cross examining witnesses, mention these people. Even the Apostle himself knowing his life was full of challenges that you can use as part of your prayer of supplication says in 1 Corinthians 11 vs.1

Follow my example, as I follow the example of Christ.

My wife and I have had many instances where we had to use the prayer of supplication in order to get a miracle. We have used this kind of prayer for our family, our ministry and in business and it works every time.

Paul was victorious and through this revelation of supplication you shall experience the same victory. If you can just get a hold of what God is saying to you through these pages, you shall pray for the impossible and get positive results!

Key issues to reconsider when you must have a miracle

1. The prayer of supplication is based on merits for it to be considered for where the merits are weak like in a court of law the case will be thrown out by the judge. In other words the prayer will not be heard.
I heard of a man who was on trial for the murder of his wife once. The investigators having found among tones of evidence his fingerprints all over the gun concluded that he was the perpetrator. The wife had been shot with one fatal bullet to the head, she died instantly. He claimed someone else had planted a gun in the boot of his car and it went off by itself and shot his wife who so happened to be passing by. He had no explanation on how his finger prints were all over the murder weapon. What a story! Because of the tallness of his tale and lack of any evidence in his defense the case was not heard for even a day. The judge decided to make a ruling straightaway and that ruling was guilty. You see, his case had no merit and the judge decided not to waste time listening to him.

    Your prayer of supplication will not be heard if it has no merit.

2 The merits are based on the strength of the case or arguments. This essentially involves bringing the Lord into remembrance of his word concerning the matter on hand.

3 For one to be able to present strong merits, one needs a clear and concise understanding of the logos (written word) of God. This understanding comes from an intimate relationship with God through prayer. One needs '**kratos**' power, which is one of the supernatural powers of a believer. This is basically the power of invincibility based on the word of God. It is the level of immunity to all possibilities of failure, defeat, poverty and hurt. This comes from meditating upon God's word until the spoken words do not depart from ones mouth. (for more detailed teachings on this see my book Supernatural Power Of The Believer)

4 This kratos power (power of the word) will enable one to present an argument based on the word back to God as a basis of supplication, where one is not aware of such a right or the relevant word to bring God in remembrance ones supplication may not be heard for it will seize to be a supplication since it lacks merits. God's word is the merit.

See the word says;

And ye shall know the truth, and the truth shall make you free.
John 8 vs. 32

So if one does not know the truth – in any matter under consideration you can never be made free, for the truth you know is what makes you free. It's not just the truth that makes you free then, it is the truth you know.

So if you do not know the word, how then will you present your case or strong arguments? If your kratos power (power of the word) is weak, your merits will be weak and your supplications or deesis will be thrown out without being heard. If you don't know what rightfully belongs to you according to the word of God, you can never experience all God has provided for you.

4 Whilst you are presenting the word back to God, who John 1 vs.1 defines as the word itself, this should be done in humility, honour and respect.

The Power of Supplication – deesis – in healing

Watch this;

In those days was Hezekiah sick unto death. And Isaiah the prophet the son of Amoz came unto him, and said unto him, Thus saith the LORD, Set thine house in order: for thou shalt die, and not live.

Then Hezekiah turned his face toward the wall, and prayed unto the LORD, And said, Remember now, O LORD, I beseech thee, how I have walked before thee in truth and with a perfect heart, and have done that which is good in thy sight. And Hezekiah wept † sore. Then came the word of the LORD to Isaiah, saying, Go,

Supplication - Requests and Arguments

and say to Hezekiah, Thus saith the LORD, the God of David thy father, I have heard thy prayer, I have seen thy tears: behold, I will add unto thy days fifteen † years. And I will deliver thee and this city out of the hand of the king of Assyria: and I will defend this city.

And this shall be a sign unto thee from the LORD, that the LORD will do this thing that he hath spoken; Behold, I will bring again the shadow of the degrees, which is gone down in the sun dial of Ahaz, ten degrees backward. So the sun returned ten degrees, by which degrees it was gone down. The writing of Hezekiah king of Judah, when he had been sick, and was recovered of his sickness:
Isaiah 38 vs. 1-9.

The moment King Hezekiah received the prophetic word from Isaiah he 'turned his face towards the wall' which shows humility, as he prayed by way of supplication he immediately presented his case based on his merits.

This case also satisfies the four points of a legal argument;

The statement of conclusion or prayer request being healing, and long life, Hezekiah showed humility by facing the wall in supplication. He placed God in remembrance of what he had done as a king to God's people.

King Hezekiah had walked in truth and with a perfect heart and had done that which is good in God's sight. According to God's word, King Hezekiah had no reason to have a short life or be in sickness. For obedience to God's word was enough to gain God's favor and blessings.

The word prayer used in Isaiah 38;2 comes from the Hebrew root word **'palal'** which means to make supplication – to intervene , interpose, to pray, entreat.

However in the case of Hezekiah he gave citation of God's word implicitly. He gave a citation or brought God into remembrance of what he had done as per God's word. In other words Hezekiah was a doer and not a hearer of God's word and from his deeds he had a legal standing before God to cite his deeds, which is similar to citing his word.

The prayer achieved immediate results, and God responded by giving the prophet a word that he would be healed and his days were also going to be increased by fifteen years.

You see crying only does not work as some believers think. The tears of Hezekiah were seen by the Lord but more importantly it was the supplication by way of merits presented.

We observe that Moses' merits were based on the word, more specifically a covenant God entered with Abraham, in the case of Hezekiah his merits were based on his deeds or rather being a doer of the word. If supplication can be used in the supernatural like applied by the early church, used in health and protection it sure can be used in finances by applying the very same principles.

Supplication - deesis over Finances

Deuteronomy 26 talks about offerings of first fruits and tithes, how it is to be removed and taken to the Levites, the Priests. It details how the Priest will take it to the altar and offer it as burnt offerings.

The conclusion of the chapter is very profound for the Prophet Moses instructs the children of Israel on how to speak over their tithe and first fruits as a way of supplication.

Then you shall say before the Lord your God; I have removed the holy tithe from my house, and also have given them to the Levite, the stranger, the fatherless, and the widow, according to all your commandments, I have not transgressed your commandments nor have I forgotten them.

Look down from your holy habitation, from heaven, and bless your people Israel and the land, which you have given us, just as you swore to our fathers, "a land flowing with milk and honey".
Deuteronomy 26 vs.13 -15.

It is important to note that the Prophet Moses who had an intimate relationship with God, the one with the audacity and boldness to tell God to repent from his anger and remind God of his covenant is teaching the children of Israel how to speak over their tithe and offering by way of supplication, the merits being;

A humble submission to the Lord that one is a doer of the word, by way of observing the tithe and first fruit commandment, a reminder that one has not transgressed the commandment nor have they forgotten them.

A humble submission to the Lord to look down and bless them and bringing God into remembrance of the covenant he swore to their fathers – a direct reference to the Abrahamic covenant and blessings.

The merits are based not only on bringing Gods word back to him but also showing how one has been a doer of the word then humbly requesting the promise that comes with doing the word.
It is an open secret that tithing and offering cause God to rebuke the devourer and also causes the windows of heaven to be open. Why not use that very scripture and use the promise of God with regards to tithing and offering over your finances by applying the same principals, which have been revealed in this chapter. For the avoidance of doubt this is the promise of God concerning tithes and offerings;

Bring all the tithes into the storehouse, that there may be food in My house, and try Me now in this
Says the Lord of hosts,
If I will not open for you the windows of heaven and pour out for you such blessing that there will be no room enough to receive it. And I will rebuke, the devourer for your sakes, so that he will not destroy the fruit of your ground, nor shall the vine, fail to bear fruit for you in the field, Says the Lord of hosts;

Supplication - Requests and Arguments

Malachi 3 vs.10-11.

...'try me now on this'...

This is very much an invite to bring forth a petition and take the promise back to him in the event one has been faithful with tithes and offerings. Speak life into your finances by making a petition for your financial needs by taking the word back to the Covenant keeping God. Try him on this and you will see the power of supplication in your finances.

I remember a time when we had a great need in our ministry for transportation. We were finding it difficult to ferry equipment to services and ministry vehicles were very few in those days in comparison to the huge size of the church and the work that needed to be done.

I remember vividly talking to the Lord about this as I humbly put in my petition basing it on his word and everything he had promised for our ministry.

A few days later a man brought a New Shape ML Mercedes Benz as a gift to the church. As if that was not enough he came again and gave a BMW 7 series. This is all happened without announcing to our partners or anybody what we needed. In fact this man came all the way from out of the country.

Shortly after that our Miracle TV offices in the UK received free of charge two equally prestigious vehicles. In the days that followed three more cars were given to the ministry and two trucks came as a bonus to these gifts. Within days nine cars had been given to the ministry from people from different walks of life who knew nothing of the need we had. They had not heard any announcement that we were in need but through the power of favor and supplication, what seemed to be impossible became possible. We got a miracle at all cost!

Now I want you to always remember the principal of humility when you contend with the Almighty. On this note we are reminded of Job 40 vs.2.

Shall the one who contends with the Almighty correct Him? He who rebukes God, let him answer it.

Bringing ones strong case should never be done as a way to vent frustrations, rebukes in a bid to correct the Almighty. The supplications must be made in humility, respect and honour the same way one makes an appeal in a court. However we have an Advocate and the Holy Spirit, which aids us in prayer and supplication.

We have an Advocate

In supplication a new covenant believer has an Advocate with the father, Jesus Christ the righteous. In this case the Judge acts as God and the devil is the accuser of the brethren so your real case is with the devil but your appeal is to God.

1 John 2 vs.1

My little children, these things write I unto you, that ye sin not. And if any man sin, we have an advocate with the father, Jesus Christ the righteous.

An advocate is a lawyer who pleads your case but any lawyer or advocate acts under instruction of the supplicant (you). Which is why it is important for the supplicant to know what to instruct and also, this is why we pray in the name of Jesus Christ our advocate. Where the supplicant is not aware of his rights to an advocate or right to bring his case and argument before the Lord so that one may be acquitted he will not be able to have supplications heard or prayers received. However if you are bold, confident and use his word to the advocate to plead your case in the father's court victory is certain.

The accuser of the brethren, the devil will not go down without a fight; he will always be out to poke holes in our merits, arguments and supplications.

Revelation 12 vs.10

And I heard a loud voice saying in heaven, Now is come salvation, and strength, and the kingdom of our God, and the power of his Christ; for the accuser of our brethren is cast down, which accused them before our God day and night.

Satan heads a kingdom, with wicked spirits in high places, he has rulers of darkness, powers and principalities out there to take advantage of any holes in our merits, arguments, deeds or mistakes. But we have an armor of God to protect us and also attack Satan and his cohorts. The word, prayer and supplication are what we have as tools on the offensive.
Ephesians 6 vs.13-18

Wherefore take unto you the whole armour of God that ye may be able to withstand in the evil day, and having done all, to stand. Stand therefore, having your loins girt about with truth, and having on the breastplate of righteousness; And your feet shod with the preparation of the gospel of peace; Above all, taking the shield of faith, wherewith ye shall be able to quench all the fiery darts of the wicked. And take the helmet of salvation, and the sword of the Spirit, which is the word of God: Praying always with all prayer and supplication in the Spirit, and watching thereunto with all perseverance and supplication for all saints;

So in supplications you are praying God's own word, so how then can he deny his own word, which he has placed above himself?

The Accuser in Action

See how the devil accuses the brethren in a bid to poke holes in ones merits in the book of Job.

Job 1 vs.6

Now there was a day when the sons of God came to present themselves before the Lord, and Satan also came among them.

And the Lord said to Satan, 'from where do you come?' So Satan answered the Lord and said, 'from going to

and fro on the earth, and from walking back and forth on it'.

Then the Lord said to Satan 'Have you considered My servant Job that there is none like him on the earth, a blameless and upright man, one who fears God and shuns evil'.

So Satan answered the Lord and said 'does Job fear God for nothing, have you not made a hedge around him, around his household and around all that he has on every side. You have blessed the work of his hands and his possessions have increased in the land.

'but now stretch out your hand and touch all that he has and he will surely curse you to your face.

It's important to note that to stand before God; the devil was using Adamic authority he gained when he deceived Adam and Eve so as to gain access. He was using this same Adamic authority so as to accuse Job and poke holes into the hedge God had laid over him and his household possessions.
The merits Job had on his arguments were that he was a doer of the word – he was upright, blameless, shunned evil and above all feared God.

Instead of Job making a supplication unto the Lord based on his deeds Job confessed fear and this is how the accuser gained access through the hedge God had laid around him.

Job 3 vs.24
For my sighing comes before I eat, and my groaning's pour out like water.
For the thing I greatly feared has come upon me. And what I dreaded has come upon me.
I am not at ease, nor am I quiet; I have no rest, for trouble comes.

Fear breaks the hedge around believer's lives; it weakens our merits and arguments before the Lord.

2 Timothy 1 vs.7
For God has not given us the spirit of fear; but of power, and of love, and of a sound mind.

The root word for 'sound-mind' is the word ***sophronismos***, which translates to self – control, moderation, an admonishing or calling to soundness of mind. This is the soundness of mind required in making supplications, a mindset and an understanding of supernatural laws. Where one submits an argument either based on the word, promises of God or presenting an account of being a doer of the word. Self-control is required as a call for humility as these submissions have to be put forth humbly.

The risks of living in fear are shown in the book of proverbs.
The fear of a man brings a snare, but whoever trusts in the Lord shall be safe.
Proverbs 29 vs.25

Fear pokes holes in ones faith and fear itself is the direct opposite of faith. It opens a door which the accuser will take advantage of just like he did Job. Ones merits become compromised when one operates from the position of fear. You will not be able to come with boldness with your petition and argument for fear compromises your confidence. You would have created a snare; a trap for yourself which means your supplications will not be heard.

My wife and I once met a lady who was so distraught with fear. Her firstborn child committed suicide some years before we met her and since then, she lived her life in fear thinking something was lurking around the corner just waiting to pounce on the rest of the family. She stopped living. She lost her position at a very prestigious bank, her marriage was strained and the rest of her children just seemed to be on a downward spiral. You see, this is the same fear Job had. He gave way for the devil to break the hedge around his life and this is exactly what this woman had done. Listen, the word of God says;

But whoever listens to me will dwell safely, and will be secure, without fear of evil
Proverbs 1 vs.33

Job did not listen to the Lord in terms of prayer of supplication, hence did not dwell safely because the accuser, the devil perforated his hedge by taking advantage of his confession of fear of evil.

Praying for the Impossible

The book of Genesis in chapter 32 gives us an encounter between Esau and Jacob; this was after Jacob had served time working for Laban for years after he had swindled the firstborn birthright from his brother.

Jacob tried to make peace by sending messengers to his brother with gifts but Esau was already on his way with 400 men coming to where Jacob had camped. When Jacob learnt of this move he was greatly afraid and distressed but instead of confessing his fear and living in fear Jacob chose to supplicate.

Then Jacob said, 'O God of my father Abraham and God of my father Isaac, the Lord who said to me, "Return to your country and to your family, and I will deal well with you";
I am not worthy of the least of all the mercies and of all the truth, which you have shown your servant; for I crossed over this Jordan with my staff, and now I have two companies.
Deliver me, I pray, from the hand of my brother, from the hand of Esau, for I fear him, lest he come and attack me and the mother with the children.
For You said, 'I will surely treat you well, and make your descendants as the sand of the sea, which cannot be numbered for multitude'
Genesis 32 vs. 9-12

Whilst Jacob was in fear of his brother just like Job, he did something about his fear, he went on to make a supplication unto the Lord and he presented his strong case.

Be Anxious for Nothing

The Apostle Paul sums it up this way in his letter to the Philippians.

Be anxious for nothing, but in everything by prayer and supplication, with thanksgiving, let your requests be known to God.
Philippians 4 vs.6

The word anxious is from a Greek root word *merimnao*; it means to be troubled with cares, which really is rooted in fear. Instead of operating in fear you need a sound mind, where you listen to the word of God, and let your requests be known to God. The requests need supplication, which involves you presenting strong arguments but this alone requires you to be aware of God's word in order for you to present it back to him. The presentation ought to be done as a way of bringing God into remembrance of his word, his promises or the works or deeds that you have done. Remember that all this should be done in humility but with the confidence that you have an advocate in Jesus Christ.

Supplication - deesis results in the Supernatural

For you to see what supplication can do for you look at how the church applied it when some of its key members were arrested. **Acts 4 vs.1-22** says tells us this story.

Peter and John had been arrested for preaching about the Lord Jesus Christ and the resurrection from the dead. The Rulers,

Praying for the Impossible

High priests, Elders and Scribes thought the only way to stop them from spreading the word further was to threaten them against speaking or teaching the name of Jesus.

Not only were the rulers trying to fight a name above all names but they were trying to fight notable and tangible results of using the name of Jesus – for a notable miracle of healing had taken place and even they couldn't deny it.

The only thing they managed to do was to further threaten them before letting them go. They found no way of punishing them for fear of the crowds who were now glorifying God for what had been done.

Now watch how they applied supplication and you can follow their example because this is the thing that will get you to get your prayers answered at all cost. Look at this;

And being let go, they went to their own companions and reported all that the chief priests and elders had said to them.
So when they heard that, they raised their voice to God with one accord and said; 'Lord, You are God, who made heaven and earth and the sea, and all that is in them, who by the mouth of your servant David have said;
"Why do the nations rage, and the people plot vain things? The kings of the earth took their stand, And the rulers were gathered together against the Lord and against His Christ."

For truly against Your holy Servant Jesus, whom You anointed, both Herod and Pontius Pilate, with the Gentiles and the people of Israel, were gathered together to do whatever Your hand and Your purpose determined before to be done.
Now Lord, look on their threats, and grant to your servants that with all boldness they may speak Your word, 'by stretching out your hand to heal and that signs and wonders may be done through the name of your holy Servant Jesus.
And when they had prayed, the place where they were assembled together was shaken; and they were all filled with the Holy Spirit, and they spoke the word of God with boldness.
Acts 4 vs.23-31

Notice how they started their supplication – it was by telling God what he created, showing Him his greatness by way of glorifying, magnifying and worshipping Him, which shows us humility, honour and respect in supplication. This is the same pattern you ought to use with your own supplication if you are to achieve results for the impossible.

The Accuser of the brethren did not fold his arms and watch, the devil and his cohorts sort to instill fear by way of threats and intimidation tactics so as to prevent the use of the name of the Lord Jesus. Thank God for supplication led by Peter and John for they overcame the threats and achieved great tangible results. You can have the same results today but you ought to know what God said in his word. Read his word and outline his promises and your problem will sure vanish before your eyes. The devil himself is afraid of supplication and is defeated by it.

Now if you look again at the supplication in Acts 4 vs.23 the petition was for boldness to speak the word and also about having power exactly as the word concurs in **1 Corinthians 4 vs.20:**

For the Kingdom of God is not in word, but in power.

These guys were not just after a lot of talk; their message was not about wise and persuasive words but demonstration of God's power. The word power above is from the root word **dunamis** which is a force; specifically miraculous power, it's an ability or strength to perform miracles. It is the dynamic ability to cause changes to every situation. Together with **kratos** highlighted earlier, **dunamis** is also one of the dimensions of the supernatural power of a believer.

Notice their specific petition for **dunamis**;

Acts 4 vs.30
'...by stretching out your hand to heal and that signs and wonders may be done through the name of your holy Servant Jesus...

The petition was for necessities and basics, which are required for preaching the word and their merits were based on the word of God. Consistent with supplications, put God in remembrance of his word.

Supplication - Requests and Arguments

They placed God in remembrance with this;

"Why do the nations rage, and the people plot vain things? The kings of the earth took their stand, And the rulers were gathered together against the Lord and against His Christ."
Acts 4 vs. 25-26

This verse is actually an extract of a scripture in **Psalms 2 vs. 1-2**. Taken as verbatim, this is exactly what you must do as a believer. Writing down your petition backed by specific and relevant scripture is paramount, for it strengthens your strong reason and argument. These people knew they needed to present a strong case before God as they supplicated. So they simply found a scripture that covered their case in the book of Psalm 2 vs. 1-2 and quoted it back to God exactly as it appears in the word and their case was heard.

The supplication achieved immediate results, for we serve a Covenant keeping God who answereth by fire. In no time the place was shaking and they were filled with the Holy Spirit and they spoke the word with boldness. And the demonstration of Power they petitioned came shortly thereafter in Acts 5.

And through the hands of the apostles MANY SIGNS AND WONDERS were done among the people. And they were all with one accord in Solomon's Porch.
Acts 5 vs.12.

These are tangible results of supplication which one cannot fight or argue with.

Our Confidence and Faith in our Petitions

**And this is the confidence that we have in him, that if we ask any thing according to his will, he heareth us; And if we know that he hear us, whatsoever we ask, we know that we have petitions that we desired of him.
1 John 5 vs.14-15.**

The will of the Lord is his word, and if our supplications (petitions) – case, merits and strong arguments are according to his word we have a confidence that will build up our faith that what we have requested in our supplication will be heard. Our faith is build up, for it is the evidence of things hoped for, the evidence of things not seen. The word of God becomes proof to you and to the accuser that you have what you have petitioned.

The will of God has been made clear; in terms of the order of our requests that we must start with supplications then prayers, intercessions and finally thanksgiving. We also noted that supplications are weighed based on the merits of arguments presented, which have to be consistent with God's word (Will). This will come from reading; studying and meditating upon the word of God, for one will find scriptures that you know will fit your petition.

When you write your petitions down, based upon the word of God, you establish the will of God, when you pray it aloud, you build up your faith in what you already know for faith cometh by hearing, and hearing by the word of God. Remember, without faith it is impossible to please God.

This is how we must pray, when we are praying for the impossible – **IT TAKES SUPPLICATION - Deesis.**

CHAPTER THREE

Supplication – Gaining access to supplicate – Approach, Attitudes, Gestures and Words

In the court system there is a way or order which is used to gain access. This is usually expressed in the form of gestures and language.

The words 'all rise' are issued by the court bailiff to ensure everyone stands on their feet as the judge enters the court room. This implies everyone is expected to be seated and wait for the judges' appearance. Standing up is a sign of respect and people have to wait for the judge to sit before they are asked to sit. Even when one leaves the court room whilst court is in session, one is expected to bow their head towards the Judge as one leaves.

The Judge is addressed as 'Your Honour, Your Worship, My Lord' depending on country or jurisdiction but the principal of gaining access to supplicate remains the same. It is done with honour and expressed in the way we address the judiciary or our attitude towards them.

Failure to adhere to the court conduct will result in one being charged with contempt of court. You will remember that I mentioned earlier that being held in contempt essentially means an order which declares a person or legal persona to have disobeyed or been disrespectful of the court's authority, this may result from a failure to obey a lawful order of a court, showing disrespect for the judge, disruption of the proceeding through poor behavior or acts which may be deemed likely to jeopardize a fair trial. The order is the judges' strongest power to impose sanctions for acts which disrupt the court process. The judge may impose a fine or even jail term depending on the severity of the contempt.

Your appearance matters

Therefore that disciple whom Jesus loved saith unto Peter, it is the Lord. Now when Simon Peter heard that it was the Lord, he girt his fisher's coat unto him for he was naked, and did cast himself into the sea.
John 21 vs.7

Now listen, these are the Lord's disciples who already had a good relationship with him. They would eat at the same table, go to crusades together and pray together. They were intimate. These guys were the ones who were with Jesus all the time, they were his inner circle. They are the ones whom we expect could probably have gotten away with being naked before him but they respected him too much to be seen not looking the right way. As soon as Simon Peter heard that Jesus was approaching, (having stripped while he was in the water) rushed to grab his coat so he could cover himself and be appropriate before his savior and King.

Supplication – gaining access to supplicate – Approach, Attitudes, Gestures & Words

A lady from a small county in the United States was found in contempt of court for dressing inappropriately. She had been warned by her lawyer to not come to court wearing her signature short shorts but she wouldn't listen. She appeared on her first hearing wearing the shortest shorts and as soon as the judge saw her, he found her in contempt of court for inappropriate dress. She was sentenced to some time in prison.

The way you look and hold yourself shows the amount of respect that you have for God. As a child of God you cannot just dress anyhow. Do the best you can even if you don't have much. Always strive to respect God by respecting yourself especially when it comes to your appearance. If Simon Peter saw it fit to first cover himself appropriately before approaching the Lord Jesus yet he was one of his disciples why shouldn't you? The book of 1 Corinthians 6 vs.19-20 says it this way;

Or do you know that your body is a temple of the Holy Spirit within you, whom you have from God? You are not your own, for you were bought with a price. So glorify God in your body.

As you present your case in the courts of the Almighty God, do not be found in contempt of court by the way you appear or hold yourself. As stated in the above scripture, your body should glorify God. Treat yourself with respect, it simply shows you also respect God.

So in order to gain access to a court system you must not only show respect in gestures or attitudes but must express it in words and even in writing of arguments.

Psalms is very instructive in this regard;

Psalm 100 vs. 2-5
Serve the Lord with gladness, come before his presence with singing. Know ye that the Lord is God; it is he that hath made us, and not we ourselves, we are his people, and the sheep of his pasture. Enter into His gates with thanksgiving, And into His courts with praise. Be thankful to Him, and bless His name". For the Lord is good, his mercy is everlasting and his truth endureth to all generations.

This is how we gain access into his gates and court – the keys are thanksgiving, praise, blessing him by giving him glory and worshipping Him. In much the same way one is found in contempt if one does not praise and honour the courts, our supplications run the risk of being in contempt if we do not give God glory, thanksgiving and bless him.

In aeronautical and astronautical engineering the direction of an aircraft to the horizon is referred to as attitude. The direction and altitude of the plane is all determined by its attitude control systems.

The same is true in your prayer life, what is your attitude towards prayer, is it about a relationship, a fellowship and intimate relationship with the Father or have you reduced prayer into a begging session? You see, God is not an errand boy or butler whom you send to fetch things for you upon request. No, he is way too big for that. An attitude of humility is very important in building a relationship with the father which will result in effective prayers for the impossible.

Supplication – gaining access to supplicate – Approach, Attitudes, Gestures & Words

The Our Father prayer that Jesus taught his disciples in Matthew Chapter 6 was simply an example or an outline on how to pray. If you examine this prayer while you read it, you will observe an incredible **relationship** that has been built up between the Son and his Father. You will also see not only **communication and conversation** between the two, but also much **honor and praise** that is being given, **forgiveness** that is being requested, complete **trust** being placed in the Father's hands, the **recognition of incredible power**, the **awareness of great glory**, and the **proclaiming of supreme authority**.

Matthew 6 vs. 9-13
Our Father in heaven, Hallowed be Your name.
Your kingdom come. Your will be done on earth as it is in heaven.
Give us this day our daily bread.
And forgive us our trespasses, as we forgive those who trespass against us.
And lead us not into temptation, but deliver us from evil. For Yours is the kingdom and the power and the glory forever. Amen

If you are going to take the time to say your supplications, then the supplications that you say should come from the deepest part of your heart, which reflects an intimacy, a relationship and fellowship with God. So talk to him **in detail** about your needs – your supplications, hopes, dreams, joys, and everything else that is having any kind of importance or effect on your life.

Prayer is our lifeline to God.
We should tell God our thoughts, desires, hurts, and problems, as well as giving him our thanks and praises. He wants to hear them all from us. He already knows what they are but he wants us to tell them to him. Also remember that God's help may come about in steps or stages. Your request to the Father may involve and have impact on the lives of many, many others, both now and in the future. Therefore you may not receive immediately all that you request from him, but the tide has turned the very moment that you turned to him. Whenever you cast all of your care and concern upon him and rely upon him totally to supply your needs and to show you how you are to live, he is quick to respond.

Giving God our thanks is part of supplications

I mentioned earlier about the importance of the actual prayer of giving thanks and that it can make up part of another prayer. In the case of supplications, the prayer of giving thanks is also important. Imagine for a moment that you do something really nice for a person you care about. However that person doesn't give you the slightest recognition or acknowledgment. That person simply accepts whatever you did for them, and without a word, simply walks away. Would you be eager to do the next nice thing for that person? And if you did another nice thing, and there was again not the vaguest hint of acknowledgment or thankfulness, would you continue to do nice things for that unthankful and rather selfish person?

Supplication – gaining access to supplicate – Approach, Attitudes, Gestures & Words

God is just like us. We were made in his image and his likeness and the Bible tells us repeatedly that he is very active in our lives. We are his children, and because of his love for us, he allows many wonderful things to come into our lives each and every day. God loves to bless his children, and if you consider that God is almighty and that nothing in this world happens without his permission, then those wonderful things that happen to you in the course of a day, have to be allowed by God. In your prayer of supplication, thanking God and acknowledging him as your source for everything is important. It should be part of your prayer of supplication.

There are many a time that God engineers things like giving you that extra second that you needed which prevented a terrible car crash. Could God be behind that warm and loving memory that gives you such incredible peace and joy? Was God the guiding force that assembled your family? Does God make sure your health, and the health of your love ones, stays excellent? Was it God that got you through school and guided the way to your employment? Was God the one responsible for softening your hardened heart so that you became aware of his glorious presence? Is God the one giving you that extra strength that enables you to endure that trial or tribulation? Is God the one behind the effort to get you to lead a Godly life which will guide you up to, and through the gates of his paradise?

Do you see how much God has already done for you? Many people would simply pass all of the above off as pure luck and that God is not involved in any of it. The blessings will definitely not continue if God is not acknowledged. The book of Psalm says;

Psalm 95:2
Let us come into his presence with thanksgiving; let us make a joyful noise to him with praise.

And Apostle Paul goes on to say;

Hebrews 13:15
Therefore, let us continually offer to God the sacrifice of praise, that is, the fruit of our lips, giving thanks to His name."

There is an elderly lady I heard of once who knew just how to come into God's presence full of thanksgiving in her heart. She would shout the most in church and dance the most despite her age. Even as the preacher took to the pulpit to preach, she would not sit down eagerly waiting in anticipation of what the word was going to be that day. The entire preaching would be chorused with her regular praises and thanksgiving to God. You see, such a person would never struggle to build a case before God.

If we take a look at a man after God's own heart in the book of Psalms we get a good example of how David executed his supplications. He would start off with **thanksgiving**, **glorifying God** and then bring in his petition in one verse and straight after that he would revert back into **thanksgiving and praising God**. The whole chapter from verse one of Psalms 118 to verse 29 is all about giving praise and thanksgiving. The petition is only found in verse 25 as follows;

Supplication – gaining access to supplicate – Approach, Attitudes, Gestures & Words

Save now, I pray, O Lord, O Lord I pray, send now prosperity.

His supplication was not just about demands, he knew how to be after God's own heart, how to have a finger on God's pulse. He gave thanks before and just after his supplications, he did not need to wait for the physical manifestation of the request because he had trust in God and had an intimate relationship with him.

Notice the words of Jesus;

Therefore I say unto you. What things soever you desire, when ye pray, believe that ye receive them, and ye shall have them.
Mark 11 vs.24

Notice when you are supposed to believe you have received – it's when you pray not when you have seen the results or when they manifest in the physical, it's when or as you pray. Now if you believe you have received when you pray, surely thanksgiving should be done the moment your supplication has been made known. That shows spiritual maturity and faith.

Supplication - deesis – Humility and Worship

One major aspect in the approach to supplication is an attitude of humility and worship. Now humility is the one virtue that once you think you have it, you've lost it. You can't claim, oh, I love my humility! I'm so humble! It doesn't work that way, no. Watch those people that brag about their humility!

James begins to address this in chapter 4 vs.1-5,

What is causing the quarrels and fights among you? Isn't it the whole army of evil desires at war within you? You want what you don't have, so you scheme and kill to get it. You are jealous for what others have, and you can't possess it, so you fight and quarrel to take it away from them. And yet the reason you don't have what you want is that you don't ask God for it. And even when you do ask, you don't get it because your whole motive is wrong- you want only what will give you pleasure.

You can't just tag on some little phrase to a prayer and say it at a certain time of the day or do something like that and think that is particularly going to get God's ear. You know what gets God's ear? It is when our hearts and our motives are pure when we pray and we genuinely and truly want His will and way in our life.

These aspects above show that there are obstacles to sincere supplication in our prayers. Remember Paul's words:
For the flesh lusts against the Spirit and the Spirit against the flesh; and these are contrary to one another, so that you do not do the things that you wish.
Galatians 5:17 NKJV

This shows us that obstacles such as our own flesh can affect supplications. For us to be humble in our supplications we have to break the flesh.

Supplication – gaining access to supplicate – Approach, Attitudes, Gestures & Words

In the flesh we are ambitious. We dream, plan, and strive with all our might to achieve our dreams whether it is a lovely home with a white picket fence, two cars in the garage, and children playing. Or the dreams may be to rise in our vocation or profession and achieve things we can be proud of. In our spirit too many of us think that we have to poor mouth in prayer. Being humble before God doesn't mean asking Him to help you be satisfied with being a loser. Supplication caters for basic needs not luxuries.

The Apostle protests in his Philippian letter;

…put no confidence in the flesh.
Philippians 3 vs.3

You see, the flesh tends to be self-confident. Because they themselves are so able, the fleshly do not need to trust in the Holy Spirit. This does not show any humility at all.

The story of Mephibosheth is also a true sign of humility as the bible says:

And he bowed himself, and said, What is thy servant, that thou shouldest look upon such a dead dog as I am?
2 Samuel 9 vs.8

This man was meant to be the King of Israel. The word bowed, is from the Hebrew root word ***shachah***, which means to depress, prostrate (especially reflexive, in homage to royalty or God). Humbly beseech, reverence, to stoop, worship.

However for a new covenant believer who is in Christ, who has been made a King and Priest unto God who should reign on the earth, you may not refer to yourself as a dead dog but the point was to highlight the essence of humility in supplication.

As I mentioned before, in the legal court system, supplication is used as a form of appeal against mistaken verdicts and as a means of rectifying inadequate legislation. The process is done in utmost humility to the extent that the judiciary is addressed as your worship. If one does not respect and honour the court you may be found guilty of 'contempt of court' which is a charge on its own, irrespective of the merits or strength of your appeal or argument. This may result in your case being thrown out without being heard any further.

In our supplications before God worship not only forms part of humility but it is a principal that leads to romancing the heart of God. There are several forms of worship but only one (proskuneo) achieves results in supplications.

Levels of Worship

If you are going to build a case through supplication to God you need to be a true worshipper. One who understands what it means to be loved and love God in return. One of the master worshippers we know in the Bible was David and as I have already pointed, he knew how to supplicate before God.

I want you to take a look at what the bible says about worship so that you can get the essence of what worship fully involves. If you already had information on what you think worship is

Supplication – gaining access to supplicate – Approach, Attitudes, Gestures & Words

the best thing is to empty your cup so that you can receive. It is impossible to fill a cup that is already full.

I am going to highlight only a few from the bible that I know will elevate your understanding and also help when you are building your merits. These are a combination of Hebrew and Greek words that define worship. Some of the words are things we do and some things God expects from us. I have outlined these starting with ***proskuneo***.

Proskuneo

The Lord Jesus Christ says this to the woman at the well, **John 4 vs. 21-23** Jesus said to her, ***"Woman believe Me the hour is coming when you will neither on this mountain nor in Jerusalem worship the Father. You worship what you do not know; we know what we worship, for salvation is of the Jews. But the hour is coming, and now is, when the true worshippers will worship the Father in spirit and truth for the Father is seeking such to worship Him.***

The word worship is repeated a total of six times in the passages above and all have the same meaning in the Greek, which is **Proskuneo,** to kiss toward or to lean forward so as to kiss and then ends with kissing.

The book of **Matthew 2 vs. 9** speaks of the wise men,

"...When they saw the star, they rejoiced with exceeding great joy. And when they had come into the house, they saw the young Child with Mary His mother, and fell

down and worshiped Him. And when they had opened their treasures, they presented gifts to Him gold, frankincense and myrrh."

When the wise men saw their new King and savior, they worshipped Him. The gifts they gave to Him were the result of worship. We confuse between the result of worship and the spirit of worship. Some people when they come to church, they experience the power of God and His glory so much that they fall down and worship Him. As a result they are pushed to give God something. You can give those gifts in the house of God but if those gifts come from pride, worship is automatically gone out the window.

Note that the Hebrew word for worship ***shachah*** is similar to the Greek word for worship, which we are looking at now - ***proskuneo***. Both of them include the act of bowing down. This however is a brief outline of some of the levels of worship. Otherwise it takes an entire book to cover everything comprehensively!

Worshiping includes singing unto The Lord but when it is not from a humble heart, worship in its essence disappears completely.

There is a couple Papa Kenneth Hagin spoke of who were leading a worship session one time in a certain church. They had wonderful voices that could hit all the difficult notes with such ease. Everyone in the room was excited and they ululated and clapped as the couple demonstrated perfected voices in worship. After they were done singing their worship item, an old couple came up to the stage with only a guitar and they begin to sing unto the Lord. Their voices were very shaky and they certainly could not hit any high note. Some notes were out of tune but a phenomenal thing happened shortly after they started. Every single person in the room was knocked out completely under the glory of God as some wept and others knelt at the altar repenting of their wrongdoings.

See that? If worship is done in truth and in spirit – it is vindicated. If pride sets in and all we care about is hitting the right notes and sounding good to the people, the spirit of worship lifts.

The whole idea is to be humble in the presence of God. As mentioned earlier, entering the courts of God with a humble heart will ensure your case is not only heard but granted before him. You can sing, dance and shout all you like but if your motive is not right then it's wrong.

There is a man I saw once dancing as if mad in the house of the Lord. The man brought out of the bag every style of dance as he danced and danced in worship. It seemed he didn't care who was watching all he cared to do was dance for his God.

Afterwards I had people approaching me to report that they found his style of dancing 'offensive'. They wanted him to be reproached for dancing in such an offensive way! Listen, however you worship God if it is in spirit and in truth then it's correct. David danced until he became naked!

2 Samuel 6 vs. 14
"And David danced before the LORD with all his might; and David was girded with a linen ephod."
Vs. 16 goes on to say,

"...Michal Saul's daughter looked through a window, and saw king David leaping and dancing before the LORD; and she despised him in her heart."

You see David was in a deep level of worship that he didn't care about whether the handmaidens were looking or not. His wife Michal is the one who decided to be the voice of reason and advise him that what he had done was wrong. And David rightfully answered,

2 Samuel 6 vs. 21
"...It was before the LORD, which chose me before thy father... therefore will I play before the LORD.

Worshiping God is showing Him humility. The wise men showed humility as they bowed down before Him and worshipped Him.

Proskuneo is leaning forward and kissing the master's feet. It is humiliating to kiss someone's feet. You feel so small and powerless yet that's proskuneo. You are bowing down unashamedly and kissing Jesus feet.

We sometimes have some seriously powerful worship sessions in our church and demons can't help themselves but check out in such an atmosphere. We have people lying prostate on

Supplication – gaining access to supplicate – Approach, Attitudes, Gestures & Words

the ground, some laughing, some crying out to God and some lying motionless for hours. It's a tangible atmosphere where some have seen open visions while in this state. It's a deeper worship that allows you to romance the heart of God and gain access into His secrets. But you see in all this glory, there are some proud people that I have seen standing and biting their finger nails! They cannot bear to be seen looking vulnerable. Talk about insensitivity to the Spirit of God!

We are talking about how to humble ourselves before God and thus experience a close friendship with God. A close friendship is key in supplication. This is how Abraham and Moses could stand before God boldly and present their own petitions with results following immediately. They knew how to pray for the impossible with results following.

Proskuneo speaks about humbling of our heart, our mind, of changing our mindset before God and allowing Him to do whatever He sees fit in us. It is allowing him access in to our hearts and going deeper into an intimate relationship with him. As you present your supplications before God, always remember the essence of true worship. With a humble heart and the absence of fear, it becomes easy for your case to not only be heard but to be granted with positive results.

Segad

The first word in the Hebrew describing worship is **segad** - to bow before Him.

Dan. 3 vs.4
"... O peoples, nations and languages that at the time you hear the sound of the horn, flute, harp, lyre and palsertry, in symphony with all kinds of music, you shall fall down and worship the gold image that King Nebuchadnezzar has set up..."

You see the words that describe worship are different depending on the context. ***Shachah*** and ***proskuneo*** also include among other things bowing down just like ***segad***. The difference is ***segad*** means to bow down and pay respect to a notable person or somebody higher than yourself and it may not include your heart. It only physically refers to your body posture. I am sure at the time of Daniel a lot of people in Nebuchadnezzar's kingdom didn't really want to bow before those idols. They did it unwillingly out of fear. There were serious repercussions if anyone didn't bow down.

The word ***segad*** is never used in a true sense of worship to our God. This tells us that God doesn't just want our outward form, our outward worship, our physical worship or posture alone although the words ***shachah*** and ***proskuneo*** include that but they go beyond just bowing before God. Many people in church today '**segad**'. They like to show that they are close to God by their body postures. They will 'act out' true worship. God is not looking for just actions; He wants us to have a relationship with Him that allows us to gain access into His secrets. You see, God is a gentleman; He wants us to bow down to Him willingly because we love Him. It is not His intention to force anyone to love Him. We bow because we are intimate. The purpose for knowing segad is for you to be aware that as

Supplication – gaining access to supplicate – Approach, Attitudes, Gestures & Words

you seek a deeper relationship with God through worship, you cease to act out things and worship Him in truth and in Spirit.

Atsab

Atsab is a worldly form of worship. If we take a look at the book of Jeremiah it becomes clearer.

Jeremiah 44:19

"...And when we burned incense to the queen of heaven and poured out drink offerings to her, did we make cakes for her, to worship (Atsab) her, and pour out drink offerings to her without our husbands' permission?"

Here is a worldly form of worship. *Atsab* involves worshipping of things like the sun, moon and trees.

The women mentioned in the above scripture were in *Atsab*. In *Atsab* worship you worship with things. It can be an incense offering. Notice that tithes and offerings are part of our worship. As I explained the wise men gave Jesus gifts after they had worshipped Him in truth and in spirit.

Some people think that worshipping God means to give Him something. If that's our thinking, we only understand *Atsab* worship and not *shachah* or *proskuneo* worship. Some may say that they don't burn incense or include objects when they worship God in church but the fact of the matter is if we think in our heart that doing something for God or giving God something is the essence of worship, then we are reducing worship to *Atsab* worship - worldly worship. God is not after your money. He wants your life; He wants to have an intimate relationship with you. The essence of worship is love. It's not in acting like we love Him or in giving all sorts of gifts without love. When He has your life and He becomes your Lord, you automatically surrender your tithes and offerings to Him. This is the result of your relationship with God. You become a giver because you love God not as an act of worship that stands alone.

Shachah

As we have seen, **shachah** and **proskuneo** are similar, only difference being the Hebrew and Greek translation of the same reference to worship. Now let's look at the word shachah in detail.

Genesis 22 vs.5
"And Abraham said to his young men. "Stay here with the donkey, the lad and I will go yonder and worship, and we will come back to you."

The word here used is the Hebrew word *shachah*, which means to bow down yourself. Notice that it is entirely different from *segad*. *Segad* means to bow down only, whereas *shachah* means to bow down yourself. Remember we looked at Daniel chapter 3 and everyone was bowing down but it was not out of reverence but fear. They knew that if they didn't bow they would be thrown into the fiery furnace. In **Genesis 22** Abraham took the son himself; Abraham bound the son himself;

Supplication – gaining access to supplicate – Approach, Attitudes, Gestures & Words

Abraham sought to sacrifice the son Himself, God never did it for him. God simply gave the instruction and Abraham did the rest by himself. He worshipped God willingly.

It was not a forcing matter. He had gotten to a level where he trusted God enough to simply follow what he had been told willingly.

Shachah speaks of something deeper. Worship in its essence means to humble ourselves before God. If we acknowledge that we need Him and useless without Him we open doors to enter into a deeper level.

Worship is real. God is as real as you are to your- self. There is no way you can pray for the impossible and get results if you do not understand worship, no way.

Worship is in your heart. You could do *segad*, you could bow down and your heart could still have pride. You could **Atsab** or give something like the Pharisees and the Sadducees who gave things to the temple but they had pride in their hearts.

You can give God your tithes of thousands of dollars and it means nothing if your heart is proud - there is no worship. You can sing the loudest, play musical instruments, the most skillfully but if you are not humble, there is no worship.

Pride is the very opposite of the essence of worship. And God will not have any other gods before Him, for he is a jealous God.

In a nutshell, the essence of worship is a humble heart. A heart that is willing to get to know God more.

In supplications, your attitude is of utmost importance when you appeal your case and reason with the Lord. It has to be an attitude of humility, characterized by worship. Not empty outward gestures of outward, worldly worship. God cannot be fooled for he searches the heart and will not be hoodwinked by gestures and words, which do not come out of a humble heart.

You will notice with words used by Moses in supplication like *"repent from your anger"* in **Exodus 32** these were words of someone who was very humble and had an intimate relationship with God.

Exodus 3;11

And Moses said to God, Who am I, that I should go to Pharaoh and bring the Israelites out of Egypt?

'**Who am I**', are words of humility, he considered himself unfit for the task before God. His attitude was of humility but his supplication was done with boldness.

For you to pray for the impossible and achieve great results you have to have a humble heart and worship must be a lifestyle. This is the essence of being after the Lords heart. This is key in having your supplications not only being heard but having them answered for what seems impossible in your life.

CHAPTER FOUR

Men of Prayer who used supplication - deesis - and got Miracles at all cost

In its early days, Dallas Theological Seminary was in critical need of $10,000 to keep the work going. During a prayer meeting, renowned Bible teacher **Harry Ironside**, a lecturer at the school, prayed,

"Lord, you own the cattle on a thousand hills. Please sell some of those cattle to help us meet this need."

Shortly after the prayer meeting, a check for $10,000 arrived at the school, sent days earlier by a friend who had no idea of the urgent need of Ironside's prayer. The man simply said the money came from the sale of some of his cattle!

Glory be to God! Harry Ironside caught onto the revelation of supplication and used a prayer of supplication in his time of need to achieve the impossible. He used a psalm in his prayer;

For every beast of the forest is mine, and the cattle upon a thousand hills. I know all the fowls of the mountains; and the wild beasts of the field are mine. If

Praying for the Impossible

I were hungry, I would not tell thee, for the world is mine, and the fullness thereof. Will I eat the flesh of bulls, or drink the blood of goats? Offer unto God thanksgiving, and pay thy vows unto the most High: And call upon me in the day of trouble, I will deliver thee, and thou shalt glorify me. But unto the wicked God saith, What hast thou to do to declare my statute, or that thou shouldest take my covenant in thy mouth? **Psalms 50 vs.10-15.**

This psalm is so loaded let's break it down. God is inviting us to call upon Him in our time of need (**And call upon me in the day of trouble**) but He sets conditions of thanksgiving and to pay vows unto the most High (**Offer unto God thanksgiving, and pay thy vows unto the most High**) But there is a disclaimer to the wicked, that they have no right to declare his statutes, which is his word nor do they have a right to speak Gods covenant (**But unto the wicked God saith, What hast thou to do to declare my statute, or that thou shouldest take my covenant in thy mouth?**)

Is this not the contending, arguing and reasoning which God invites us to in the book of Isaiah?

Remember;

**Put Me in remembrance [remind Me of your merits]; let us plead and argue together. Set forth your case, that you may be justified (proved right, acquitted)
Isaiah 43 vs.26 AMP**

In **chapter 2** we noticed that one's arguments and merits need to be founded on God's word or statutes for them to have strong merits. The argument and merit can also be based on a promise or covenant God entered into like the case of Moses who reminded God of Abrahams covenant. In Psalm 50 we notice again his word telling us to declare His statutes and putting in our mouths his covenants. The whole point is to make the word of God come to life, to turn it from logos – a written word into rhema - a spoken word. The word of God has to jump out of the scriptures and be spoken and come alive. This way the word of God will not come back void, it will come back with results which many will deem impossible.

The word 'mouth' in Psalms 50 is from the Hebrew root word **peh** or the Greek equivalent **stoma** it means two -edged or tip of a weapon of warfare especially a sword. Your mouth is a weapon; it is a tool to achieve the impossible. So the mouth has to declare Gods word and covenants in remembrance back to Him for one to achieve much in prayers of supplication. Notice these interesting scriptures in the book of Revelation.

And he had in his right hand seven stars; and out of his mouth went a sharp two edged sword; and his countenance was as the sun shineth in his strength.

And when I saw him, I fell at His feet as dead. But He laid His right hand on me, saying to me, 'Do not be afraid, I am the first and last, I am He who lives, and was dead, and behold, I am alive forevermore, Amen. And I have the keys of Hades and of death.

Revelation 1 vs. 16-18.

Your mouth is not just for eating and drinking… No… *the word is very nigh unto thee, in thy mouth that thou mayest do it.* This is what Deuteronomy 30;14 declares and Proverbs puts it this way;

**Death and life are in the power of the tongue; and they that love it shall eat the fruit thereof.
Proverbs 18;21**

It's high time you became a doer of the word and supplicate for your needs by the use of the power of your tongue. Declare God's word to him; bring him into remembrance of his promises and covenants. Contend and reason with him, giving Him your strong merits so that you may have prayers that achieve the impossible.

Let's look at another of God's General, who used supplication to achieve the impossible.

Smith Wigglesworth, noted as the *'apostle of faith'* earlier this century, raised at least 23 people from the dead. He was a man of the word and hated the devil with a passion. He knew God's word and he had quoted the word of God back to him when he accepted the call of God upon his life. Smith Wigglesworth after his supplication for the power to do the impossible became impregnated with power and with boldness that he simply looked for dead people to raise from the dead.

Men of Prayer who used supplication - deesis - and got Miracles at all cost

This was a man of supplication. He had proof of it and no one could doubt his ability. It could be verified. The people he raised were there to be questioned. On one occasion Bishop Ronald Coady and his wife were ministering in New South Wales, Australia, in 1950 where they met a Methodist deaconess called 'Sister Mary'. She brought them large quantities of tracts to use in their crusades.

"While there, they were reading Stanley Frodsham's book, *Smith Wigglesworth, Apostle of Faith,* the incident of his raising a young woman from the dead had gripped them, and when Sister Mary came in, they read it to her, adding, 'How we should love to meet that lady!'

"She said, 'You know that lady.'

They protested that they did not, but she persisted, 'You've known her for some time. I am that lady.'

The three of them laughed together with holy joy at God's 'coincidences'. She then told them of being paralyzed from the waist down in 1922 and of being seriously ill. Wigglesworth was holding meetings in her town, and her friends urged her to let them take her to a meeting for prayer. However, she did not believe in divine healing and did not wish to be prayed for. She soon became worse and, in fact, was dying. Her friends asked if she would allow the evangelist to pray for her if they brought him to the house. She finally consented, but he was delayed. Before he arrived, she died.

Sister Mary Pople related that she went to heaven and was allowed in the throne room. She saw the Lord Jesus sitting on His throne. She saw light such as she had never seen and heard music such as she had never heard. (There are many similar accounts today of experiences such as this). Her heart was filled with rapturous joy.

As she looked at the Lord, He pointed to the doorway by which she had entered, and she knew she had to go back even if she did not want to. When she went through that door, she heard a voice that later she knew was Smith Wigglesworth's.

He was saying, 'Death, I rebuke you in the name of Jesus.'

Then he commanded Mary to live. Her eyes opened, and those who had been weeping around her bed began to rejoice. She arose and dressed, and there was a knock at the door. Some girls from her Bible study group had arrived, thinking she was dead. To their surprise and joy, Mary herself opened the door to them. She continued in the Lord's service for many years. Not only was she raised from the dead, but she was totally healed of her sickness that had been unto death and of the paralysis that had bound her for years" That was the power of supplication. His prayer of supplication to be able to perform signs, miracles and wonders was truly heard and granted!

Another African General was Papa Benson Andrew Idahosa who was born to non Christian parents, was rejected by his father for being too sickly and frail. He constantly had fainting spells as a child and it was one spell which made his parents decide it was enough and they decided to dump him at a rubbish dump, left for dead. However God used him to do mighty miracles including healing the blind and raising up over 8 known people from the dead. He took the gospel to about 123 nations in his life time, signs and wonders came with it and at times crowds would number 1 million.

As a young Christian, **Benson Idahosa** once heard his pastor say during a morning service that Christians could raise the dead in the name of the Lord Jesus Christ. He believed it with all his heart and decided to read further about it. When he read it he decided that because it's written in his word that should settle it and that was enough for him to move around on his bicycle in the city of Benin in search of a dead person to raise to life. After about five hours of hard searching he found a compound where a little girl had died a few hours before. The corpse had been cleaned and prepared for burial. He walked boldly up to the father of the dead child. "The God whom I serve can bring your baby back to life," He told him. "Will you permit me to pray for the child and bring her back to life?" The man was startled, but he agreed. With great enthusiasm, he walked into the room and up to the bed. The child was cold and dead. With strong faith in the Lord, he called on the Lord to restore the child back to life. He turned to the corpse and called it by name, "Arise in the name of the Lord Jesus Christ." Oh Glory to God! The corpse sneezed heavily, alas! The child had come back to life!

Benson Idahosa would spend long hours in prayer, worship and study of the word, he had an intimate fellowship with God and his supplications achieved much. The words 'arise in the name of the Lord Jesus Christ' are very short but achieved much. Clearly short prayers only work for one who does long prayers of intimacy and fellowship with God. If you notice the life of Jesus, he would do long hours at night in prayer then during the day he would only come to cast out demons, raise the dead and do mighty miracles by making short commands or declarations. Short prayers do not work; they only work for people who do long prayers in private closets. In your supplications, have an intimate relationship with God based on prayer and studying the word. When in need, your supplications will not need to be long, they can even be short but they will achieve great results.

Can I testify?

One of my sons was born with one kidney and that would make any father cringe in fear. It is something that will shatter all your confidence yet the peace of the Lord was upon me. The doctor told us that he saw one kidney on the scan and we boldly said no, they were two to the doctor's face. We went for further tests and the report kept coming back that they could only see one. We had peace and that peace mounted guard on our hearts that our joy in the time of trouble was full to the destruction of the devil and the devil had to remove his hand.

You see there are two things that you need to know for healing to take place. There are facts which we are told by medical practitioners and then there is truth which is in the word of God. You are the one who decides whether you want to follow the facts or follow the truth in the word of God that confirms that we were healed by his stripes.

This is why Apostle Paul puts it this way;

Wherefore take unto you the whole armour of God that ye may be able to withstand in the evil day, and having done all to stand. Stand therefore, having your loins girt about with truth...
Ephesians 6 vs.13-14

This is the first part of the whole armour of God, which is a belt we strap around our loins - why? - The belt is used to fasten the sword and when the sword is drawn from the belt for use in the art of war, the belt has to be of truth, not facts. If your belt is of facts the sword you will pull out will be confessing facts and not truth for the sword is your mouth - which is the edge of the sword that enables you confess and pray the word of God. The mouth speaks what the mouth is full of and we must confess the truth, the word of God.

However we should not have a fixation with the physical tools of warfare for we do not wrestle against flesh and blood, because in First Thessalonians Apostle Paul refers to the breastplate as of faith and love yet in Ephesians it is referred to as shield of faith.

In our supplication we held onto the truth, the word of God;

But he was wounded for our transgressions, he was bruised for our iniquities; the chastisement of our peace was upon him; and with his stripes we ARE healed.
Isaiah 53 vs.5

Who his own self bare our sins in his own body on the tree, that we, being dead to sins, should live unto righteousness, by whose stripes ye WERE healed.
1 Peter 2 vs.24

Notice, what Prophet Isaiah prophesied centuries before the coming of Jesus Christ by saying **'we are healed'** but Peter, after the prophecy was fulfilled says **'ye were healed'**. It doesn't say we are going to be healed or you should be healed nor does it say we may be healed. It says **'ye were healed'**, that is **past tense**, it has already happened, it is yours and available.

In the book of Numbers chapter 13 vs. 25-33, Joshua and Caleb who had been sent with the other 10 spies refused to accept a bad report of the Amalekites, Hittites and Amorites and brought a good report yet the other 10 spies saw the very same land, the very same giants yet brought a bad report.

Which report are you going to believe – the good report or the bad report? We held onto the good report that the healing of our son happened by the stripes Jesus Christ received on our behalf over 2000 years ago. This was the cornerstone of our supplication, our deesis, our petition, our strong argument to God – we prayed for the impossible by use of supplication and got results.

Armed with our supplication and meditating upon it, with our confession not departing our lips we went back to the doctor and the doctors holding their report were shocked to discover that two kidneys were now showing on the report. The second kidney, which had previously not appeared on his report, was miraculously appearing. On our good report we have always known and confessed our son is in divine health and as such has two kidneys.

Glory be to God, with no medicine, our son now has two kidneys – these are the results of the power of supplication – deesis, for the finger of God had touched our son.

The main reason why supplication works is that it relies on the word of God and forces one to read the word and search the scriptures. It builds faith. You cannot just copy another person's supplication; you ought to search the scriptures for yourself even after finding a copy of the supplication that is similar to the one you are making. The trick of it is for one to search the scriptures and build a case before God against the devil!

CHAPTER FIVE

Write your own Petition - deesis

The prayer of supplication is one of the most powerful prayers because it is specific and is backed by scripture. This is just no vain repetition or spontaneous prayer, you must take time to meditate over it and put it in writing. It has to be in writing for it to become real and as a sign of seriousness for one who is facing a life and death situation. It calls for boldness for you are putting God in remembrance of his word and petitioning your request based upon His word.

Watch this;
Let my supplication come before you; Deliver me according to Your word. My lips shall utter praise, when thou hast taught me thy statutes.
Psalm 119 vs.170-171.

David had profound revelation of supplication for he petitions for deliverance according to God's word. He is bringing God into remembrance of His word but as a way of gaining access to supplicate he says 'my lips shall utter praise'. Clearly this is a man who had meditated upon the statutes of the Lord and knew what it means to be 'after the heart' of the Lord.

When you petition with such boldness, as shown by David, you get an assurance that God not only hears your petition but also answers it, for you are dealing with the known will of God, which is written in his logos. The Holy Spirit, the extraordinary strategist is there to help you remember the relevant scriptures pertaining to your situation but if you have not read your bible and your understanding of it is weak you will short circuit this crucial role of the Holy Spirit.

Look at what the extraordinary strategist will do for you;

But the Helper, the Holy Spirit, whom the Father will send in My name, He will teach you all things, and bring to your remembrance all things that I said to you. John 14 vs.26

The word Helper, is from the Greek root word **parakletos,** which means an advocate, summoned to ones side or aid so as to plead another's cause before a judge, a pleader, counsel for defense, legal assistant. You see that, that legal argument continues right throughout our case of supplication where we are bringing our petition before Gods court of justice.

When you have the relevant scripture to your petition it's time to write it down and bring forth your strong arguments with boldness. Your petition has to be specific and personal, highlighting your need, that which you deemed impossible or which you had prayed for before and you thought you didn't get an answer.

You now need to meditate upon the scripture which forms the cornerstone of your petition, you can even have other scriptures to support your petition then relate the scriptures to your request. Remember to be humble; you can't give deadlines to your petition because dates and deadlines remove you from faith because you are giving a timeframe to a physical manifestation to your petition. Remember it is impossible to please God without faith so you should believe that you have received what you petitioned for because you have done it according to God's will, which is his word. Watch this verse, it's instructive to dates.

Therefore I say to you, whatever things you ask when you pray, believe that you receive them, and you will have them.
Mark 11;24

So how then can you put physical deadlines if you have received the moment you petitioned? Don't limit or confine God with deadlines for he is able to do exceeding abundantly above all that we ask or think, according to the power that work in us.
Ephesians 3;20.

I remember receiving a call late at night from one of my sons whose daughter had been hijacked and was missing. Instinctively I got my tablet and began to type in my petition.

This is just an extract and not the full version:

Petition – Supplication: Deesis;

I humbly petition for my daughter to be found – She will be found

You are All powerful and answer petitions because you are good. I exalt and Praise your name this day, you are my God!
Psalm 46, Psalms 29;4

You are the Lord God of the impossible; you are Jehovah Shammah – the Lord God who is here and the Lord God who is there - where she is.
Mark 10;27, Ezekiel 38;45

You are the Lord God who sees me and sees her; you are Jehovah EL – Roi.
Genesis 16;13

The accuser of the brethren is trying to bring your church into disrepute; he is trying to get the Lord God's name to be condemned.

Revelation 12;10, 2 Thessalonians 1;4, 2 Timothy 3;11
You will not let him win because you have made us winners, victors and more than conquerors; she is safe and will arrive safely home.

1 Corinthians 15;57, 1 John 5;4, Romans 8;37, Psalms 4;8 and Proverbs 1;33
I have an advocate, my lawyer and mediator against the accuser, Jesus Christ – You are my Lawyer, the lawyer of the church will come through for me.
1 John 2;1

I give you thanks for this miracle Lord.
Psalms 50;14, Psalms 95;2

She will be found – I prophetically declare in the name of Jesus Christ.
Ecclesiastes 8;4 and Revelation 5;10

Date and Time

Amen

In my spirit I knew it was done, I had done my short and concise supplication over the matter and I knew the Lord God would do the impossible but the response time was exceeding abundantly above what I had thought.

Within an hour from the time I completed my supplication, I received another call – this time with the good news that she was at home safely.

The Lord God had shown up, again, true to his word. Glory be to his holy name!

I will take you through a guideline and share a few more testimonies.

Guideline to your Petition

This following is a guideline of how your petition should be and it goes something like this:

Praying for the Impossible

Father, in the mighty name of Yeshua Hamashiach (Jesus Christ in the original Hebrew) I am grateful for the opportunity you have granted me to bring you into remembrance of Your precious word as I bring my strong arguments and petitions that we may reason together and I have trust and faith that my petition is granted in full.
Isaiah 43;26

I thank you father for your word which I meditate upon for I have an assurance that by being stayed upon your word, my ways are prosperous and I am in peace. I thank you father for the Holy Spirit, my comforter, intercessor, helper and extraordinary strategist who teaches me and guides me into all truth for he has brought me into remembrance of your word which I have used to underpin my supplication; **Joshua 1 vs.8, John 14 vs.26** and **Proverbs 1 vs.33**

I humbly petition You, my Lord God, the highest authority on the universe, who has seen it fit to make me joint heir with my advocate Jesus Christ and unto You my God a King and Priest so that I have reign on the earth, to you be the Glory and dominion for ever and ever.
Romans 13;1, Galatians 3;29 and Revelations 1;6.

You have the authority to decree and grant me the following specific request for relief;

1. Request one.
   Verse(s) that relates to request one.

2 Request two.
   Verse(s) that relates to request two.

3 Request three.
   Verse(s) that relates to request three.

4 Request four.
   Verse(s) that relates to request four.

I thank you Father for the anointing of the Holy Ghost, which gives me the unction to function and the ministry of angels for there shall be no delay and any hindrance or influence from the devil and his cohorts shall be crushed by the anointing. For Satan was defeated and was made a public spectacle and has no authority or influence over me or my requests. Therefore I am not anxious for anything for I cast all my cares upon you and have made my request known according to your word. I know you have heard my requests and have answered them with a Yes and Amen.
1 John 2;20, Matthew 4;11, Matthew 26;53, Colossians 2;5, Philippians 4;6, 1 Peter 5;7, 2 Corinthians 1;20 and John 14;13.

I thank you, for you always hear my supplications, I thank you Father for this life of Zoe that you have given me and my family, an abundant life of divine health, divine joy, divine wisdom, divine peace, divine protection and divine prosperity. **John 11; 42 and John 10;10.**

In the mighty name of Yeshua Hamashiach, I supplicate, Amen.

You may want to put a date and your name and signature, then file it. The date of the petition is for a record, you may want to monitor your petitions against their physical manifestations but remember our focus is not on the physical realm for the petition is granted upon request, by faith. A record is also good for it will form a basis of your testimony.

Now, how then can you fail to achieve the impossible? This will boost and build you, to your most holy faith. Now begin to act upon your faith, talk and act as one who has received a note of victory in your spirit. Act upon what you believe, act upon your petition, begin to thank God, praise him and worship him as you supplicate. Begin to imagine your testimony before the church, how you are going to wave your testimony glorifying God on how fast your petition was heard and manifested in the physical. Begin to frame the words of your testimony for you overcome by the word of your testimony. Your vocabulary must change for your confession is as one who already possesses your requests, for faith is in the now, not in the past tense. You can read your petition over and over again, meditating it and declaring it into your spirit.

Remember your confidence in your petition;

And this is the confidence that we have in him that, if we ask any thing according to his will, he heareth us;

And if we know that he hears us, whatsoever we ask, we know that we have the petitions that we desired of him. 1 John 5 vs.14 – 15.

According to his will, is essentially His word, for the word 'will' is the word **thelema** in the Greek, which means commands, precepts, a determination, purpose, decree. It doesn't mean if he wants to give you or not, the question is, is it according to His word?

So if your petition is according to his word, then you should know that he heard it and you should know that you have the petition. The word 'know' which is used twice in verse 15 is from the Greek root word **eido** – to be aware, to perceive with understanding, which is a verb used in past tense, so your knowing is done, you have it, it's not you are going to have it but it's done already. It means to be aware, behold, be sure; it's to come to an awareness, to awaken to the reality that it is done. So you should act accordingly, for it's a knowledge that it is done, not knowledge that it's going to be done.

I know your request will be answered because before you had not used the right order of prayer nor had you used the appropriate prayer for the task on hand.

This is the prayer for you to use when praying for the impossible – Prayer of supplication will get you a miracle at all cost.

One of my sons whom I taught about **supplication over finances** applied the revelation in his business, which had been in a financial wilderness for about four years.

He meditated upon the word relating to finances and set out to write his supplication unto the lord.

Note an extract of his supplication;

To the almighty Lord God, the creator of Heaven and Earth, the supreme authority of the universe.
Genesis 1

I bring my supplication for finances according to what your word, for you said 'bring your strong reasons, let us contend together, that you may be acquitted.
Isaiah 43;26-27

I supplicate for all that you have placed under my stewardship in business, may it be fruitful, multiply, subdue and have dominion.
Genesis 1;28

I thank you for the rhema word from your prophet that this is my year of the mimshach anointing – an anointing for prosperity, for expanding, for attracting resources, for breaking limitations in my financial breakthrough, for the manifestation of God's dream which has been impregnated in my spirit to manifest and bear fruit, an anointing to be big and multiply financially. May by your grace make that anointing work for me so that I spread and expand like an outstretched wing.
Ezekiel 28;14 and 1 Samuel 16

I thank you for the rhema word from your prophet that I am a financial missionary, one who will finance the great commission, to take your gospel to the uttermost ends of the earth, to take care of the widows and orphans and to strengthen the hand of the poor so as to establish your covenant.

Matthew 28;19, Acts 1;8, Deuteronomy 8;18 and Ezekiel 16;49

Write your own Petition - deesis

I thank you for my financial wilderness, which humbled me and made me to seek you and find you. I learnt not to rely on my intelligence, wisdom, power or might and to look up to you and love you and trust in you.

Now that you are ushering me to the other side, my promised land in finances I will never forget your hand, which has delivered me and will always testify your greatness. For the power to get wealth is from you alone.
Deuteronomy 8;18, Psalm 20;7 and Isaiah 44; 24-28

I commit to tithe my increase, to give my offerings and seed into your kingdom and help the needy.

I thank you for wisdom from on high, for the opening of windows from heaven – opportunities, ideas, contacts, relationships and divine favour.
Malachi 3; 8-13 and Zachariah 1;17

Requests

1. I supplicate that the mineral rights spoken by prophecy to be sold, will be sold and commit to honour my tithe, offering and seed.

2. I pray for the resurrection of my business, that not only should it resurrect and be restored but may it bear much fruit, multiply and have dominion.

3. I supplicate that the mineral rights spoken by prophecy will begin to be mined and be fruitful, multiply and have dominion.

4 I supplicate for financial prosperity for any other business I am led into, by your spirit.
5 I supplicate for supernatural debt cancelation, supernatural resurrection of my business and supernatural prosperity.
1 Kings 17 and 2 Kings 4

I thank you for my fruitful and happy marriage, for the children you have blessed me with, may you grant me wisdom and favour to train and raise them up in the way they should go, I thank you for divine joy, happiness and health over my family. I thank you for my gift and calling as a financial missionary which was stirred and given by prophecy.
John 10;10, 1 Timothy 4;14 and 2 Timothy 1;16.

In the mighty name of Jesus Christ I pray.
Amen

Supplication after receiving a prophetic word

Though the supplication was dated early January, I had prophesied to my son a few months before – calling him by name, the first time I met him, telling him his line of business and which minerals he was mining. I told him his terrible financial status but thank God, my God reveals in order to redeem. I prophesied to him how investors would come to buy some of his claims but that would not mark his breakthrough and that some he will mine and that is when his big breakthrough will come from.

Within two months from the time of supplication, consistent with the rhema word of prophecy, his claims were sold. When he gave me his testimony it was interesting how he had discerned which ones to sell and which ones to keep for mining.

It happened as a dream of the night;

For God speaketh once, yea twice, yet man perceiveth it not. In a dream, in a vision of the night, when deep sleep falleth upon men, in slumbering upon the bed, then he openeth the ears of men and sealeth heir instruction, that he may withdraw man from his purpose, and hide pride from man.
Job 33 vs.14-17

He dreamt of a man who had died, resurrecting and telling him which claims to keep, the names of the claims were repeated three times – all he asked the man in the dream was 'how do you know I have claims in these areas?', and then he woke up. Within weeks from the dream the mineral rights he had been struggling to sell for over two years were sold, and managed to invest some of the proceeds into exploration of his remaining claims.

The results of the exploration came out, proved material deposits stretching to depths beyond he had ever imagined, which my son is now beneficiating.

Whilst a prophetic word had been given over his finances to provide guidance, every prophetic word carries an instruction and a prophetic word raises ones faith so that you act according to the guidance provided.

So the prophecy still needed prayer of supplication, for there were delays and frustrations, he still had to act upon the prophecy and supplication by looking for buyers and carrying out exploration even though the main exploration had been done prophetically.

Elijah gives us a good example about how important supplication is, even after receiving a prophetic or rhema word. A prophetic word should raise your faith but does not mean you no longer have to pray or supplicate. Elijah is described by James as a man just like us, although you and I are greater than him because The Lord Jesus said the least in the kingdom is greater than John the Baptist, whom he described as being greater than all people born of a woman. ***Matthew 11;11***.

Elijah made a prophetic declaration to King Ahab this way;

**And Elijah the Tishbite, who was of the inhabitants of Gilead, said unto Ahab, As the Lord God of Israel liveth, before whom I stand, there shall not be dew nor rain these years, but according to his word.
1 Kings 17 vs.1**

Rain did not fall for these years and do you know that you also have the supernatural power inside you to influence weather patterns. By the power of supplication the Lord God has granted us grace to stop rains during open air crusades and heavy rains stop in minutes. I also remember a time when we had an open air demonstration of power service when we supplicated that a cloud should come and cover the sun to prevent the excessive heat from affecting our service, and in minutes it happened in front of over four thousand witnesses. You also have that supernatural power not only over the weather elements but over any circumstances in your life, by supplication - deesis your miracle will come at all cost.

Elijah's supplication is revealed by James;

Elias was a man subject to like passions as we are, and he prayed earnestly that it might not rain; and it rained not on earth by the space of three years and six months.
James 5;17

When you look at the account given in the book of Kings it appears as if the prophetic word was given without prayer but the declaration came from earnest prayer. He had reasoned and contended with the Lord God in his prayers. Prophetic declarations of faith ride on the wings of earnest prayer; it is not a matter of simply declaring things without a relationship that is intimate with the Lord God.

The earnest supplication is clearer when he needed the rains back.

And it came to pass after many days, that the word of the Lord came to Elijah in the third year, saying, Go, shew thyself unto Ahab; and I will send rain upon the earth.
1 Kings 18 vs.1

Praying for the Impossible

Now that was not a prophetic declaration from the mouth of a prophet but that was the word of the Lord to Elijah. It would appear that after such a prophetic word everything is settled yet, a prophetic word exposes you to the machinations of the devil. It is time to brace for war for that prophetic word to come to pass. When the devil begins to fight your prophecy don't give up on supplication, don't doubt the rhema word of God for prophecy raises your faith but if you faint or doubt before it comes to pass you risk its fulfillment. Remember a prayer of petition is different from a prayer of faith which you must only pray once, twice or more will be equal to doubt. With supplication or your petition you can pray until your spirit signals receipt or success of your request - you will sense victory before it manifests in the physical.

An earnest prayer is heartfelt and continued, which means your spirit is deeply involved in your prayer in persistence, focused on your petition. An earnest prayer is not an emergency prayer which is quickly done in the face of adversity as a quick fix solution invariably under pressure. Such prayers do not work, short, quick fix prayers only work for those with intimate relationships with God, who have made it a habit to commune with God in long hours of praise, worship and intimate prayers.

Let us learn from Elijah; how he armed himself with the prophetic word of abundance of rain and got down to some earnest, heartfelt and continued prayer.

So Ahab went up to eat and to drink. And Elijah went up to the top of Carmel; and he cast himself down upon

Write your own Petition - deesis

**the earth, and put his face between his knees, and said to his servant, go up now, look toward the sea. And he went up, and looked, and said, there is nothing. And he said Go again seven times. And it came to pass at the seventh time, that he said, behold there ariseth a little cloud out of the sea, like a man's hand. And he said, go up, say unto Ahab, prepare thy chariot, and get thee down, that the rain stop thee not. And it came to pass in the mean while, that the heaven was black with clouds and wind, and there was a great rain.
1 Kings 18; 41-45**

When you receive a prophetic word, thank God for it is by his grace, just don't sit on it if you want it to come to pass. Act upon it, be diligent to every condition that comes with it and as it raises your faith and builds you up upon your most holy faith it should arm you with more strength to supplicate like what Elijah did. He didn't rest because God had prophesied abundance of rain; he didn't get discouraged either when his servant came back with what appeared like a bad report. He kept on sending him back as he continued to pray earnestly as he lay prostrate on the ground with his face between his knees in earnest, heartfelt and continued prayer. When a good report came with the news of a little cloud as small as a man's hand he didn't despise the early beginnings of the manifestation of his prophetic word, instead he took it as the note of victory and acted upon it by telling his servant to send word to the King. Boy I love Jesus!

Each prophecy calls for a fight and supplication is one sure weapon to ensure the word comes to pass. Fight for your prophetic word, hold fast onto your confession, act upon it and it will surely come to pass.

David was given a prophetic word and anointing by Samuel but he still had to fight a champion – Goliath and run away from Saul who sought to kill him before David could become King and sit on the throne. So even armed with a prophecy one still needs to supplicate and fight for their prophecy for it to come to pass, because the devil will not sit and watch a prophecy coming to pass.

Isaiah prophesied the coming of the Lord Jesus Christ centuries before he came, but when He came, the devil did not fold his arms to see the prophecy come to pass, King Herod sought to kill him, Joseph and Mary had to flee to Egypt with Jesus to preserve their prophesy of our savior.

Supplication works!

Thank God for these testimonies, we give glory to God for the revelation of the power in supplication.

You are next in line for a miracle. You will get a miracle at all cost, your miracle is no longer around the corner – Praying for the impossible, by supplication and acting upon what you believe is the corner.

The prayer of SUPPLICATION is the prayer for the IMPOSSIBLE. When you pray that prayer you will get a miracle at all cost.

Awaken to the revelation of **supplication – deesis**, act upon what you believe and you will surely come back with a testimony.

Lightning Source UK Ltd.
Milton Keynes UK
UKHW021018270721
387842UK00015B/1452